Key West
in Your Pocket!

Your Guide to an Hour, a Day,
or a Weekend in Key West

INSIDERS' GUIDE®

GUILFORD, CONNECTICUT
AN IMPRINT OF GLOBE PEQUOT PRESS

Contents

Welcome to Key West **4**
Planning Your Itinerary **5**
Getting Here, Getting Around **6**
Accommodations **14**
Restaurants **22**
Attractions **54**
Outdoor Recreation **85**
Arts and Culture **101**
Nightlife and Entertainment **103**
Index **115**

Welcome to Key West

Welcome to this spot on earth, perched on coral rock and limestone, with its profusion of culture, color, and fun. Only 3 miles by 5 miles, this tiny paradise packs a tropical punch for your senses. Forget the black-and-white world you left behind. When you arrive in Key West, life suddenly turns to Technicolor. By day we are the golden sun that rises over the ocean, glows brightly and then, in ardent shades of red, dips ever-so-gently beneath the Gulf horizon. As darkness enfolds, we are the cornucopia of stars that seem to gleam more brilliantly here in our endless skies than anywhere else.

Planning Your Itinerary

Key West offers a full array of activities and we give you the tools in this guide to plan your own days and nights. But first things first: remove your socks. You won't need them here. Don your shorts. They are *de rigueur*. Slip on those shades. How else can you see? And reset your watch. The pace is slower here; you're on Keys time now.

The two PopOut maps give you an overview of Key West and a detailed view of the downtown area. You'll find these maps to be an invaluable resource. Please remember that establishments may change location or close, so it's always best to call ahead.

Getting Here, Getting Around

Getting Here

Although Key West is the Florida destination of choice for thousands of visitors each year, do not expect to arrive here via commercial jetliner. Air service to this island in the sun is of the commuter variety. The planes are small, and flights are often overbooked during peak seasons, especially in January and February, so be sure to arrive early to check in for your flight. Key West International Airport (3491 South Roosevelt Blvd., Key West; 305-296-5439; www.keywestinternationalairport.com) opened a new facility in 2009.

Commercial flights are provided by the following airlines:

- **American Eagle** (American Airlines, 800-433-7300, www.aa.com): American Eagle offers connecting service to a multitude of American Airlines flights via Miami.
- **Cape Air** (305-293-0603, 800-352-0714, www.flycapeair.com): Cape Air provides scheduled service between Key West and Fort Lauderdale as well as southwest Florida airports in Naples and Fort Myers.
- **Continental Connection,** operated by Gulfstream International

Airlines (305-294-9460; 800-523-3273, domestic; 800-231-0856, international; www.gulfstreamair.com): Gulfstream provides feeder service to Key West for both Continental Airlines and United Airlines. Flights from Key West connect through Miami, Tampa, and Fort Lauderdale.

- **Delta Air Lines** (800-221-1212, www.delta.com): Comair, the Delta Connection, offers service between Key West and Atlanta, where you can pick up any number of connecting flights on Delta Airlines.
- **USAir Express** (800-428-4322, 800-943-5436, www.usair.com): USAir Express offers flights from Key West to Miami and Tampa, Florida and Charlotte, North Carolina, where you can connect with many USAir flights.

By Sea

Long a bustling port, Key West Harbor is still busy—full of commercial traffic, tourist-filled tour boats, and visiting cruise ships. If you choose to navigate your motor or sailing craft to Key West from the Atlantic, come in through the main ship channel, which is marked S.E. CHANNEL ON THE CHARTS. From the Gulf take the N.W. Channel until it intersects with the main ship channel. You can anchor out in protected areas of the harbor or put into one of the comprehensive Key West marinas.

By Car

The Overseas Highway tethers our islands to the mainland like a long umbilical cord. Addresses along this common main street are issued by mile markers, designated as MM. The highway actually curves and drifts toward the southwest, rendering it all but impossible to refer to directions as "north to here" or "south to there." Here in the Keys everything is grounded by a mile marker.

As you head toward Key West, mile marker numbers descend in order. Anyplace on the right side of the road bordering Florida Bay or the Gulf of Mexico is referred to as bayside. The opposite side of the road, bordering the Atlantic Ocean, is therefore called oceanside.

Directions to the Keys from Miami International Airport via Florida's Turnpike: Take LeJeune Road south to Highway 836 West. As you approach the ramp, get in the right-hand lane. Be aware, however, that a frontage-road access just before the sign and arrow often lures confused first-timers into turning too soon. The ramp is actually just after the sign and arrow. Follow Highway 836 West to Florida's Turnpike South, Homestead. Continue on Florida's Turnpike until it ends in Florida City at US 1. Continue south on US 1 to the Keys.

So addresses on the Overseas Highway will usually be referred to by both mile marker number and a bayside or oceanside distinction.

Parking

There are simply too many cars in Old Town Key West and too few places to put them. Patrons of the shops and restaurants in Duval Square (1075 Duval St.) will find free parking available in an adjacent lot accessed from Simonton St. Free parking for patrons of some Duval St. restaurants, shops, and bars may also be available in designated lots off either Whitehead or Simonton streets, both of which run parallel to Duval. Metered curbside parking is, of course, available on several downtown streets, including Duval, Whitehead, and Simonton, as well as along most of the streets that intersect them. Special curbside parking areas are designated for scooters and mopeds; do not leave vehicles on the sidewalk. All-day parking is available for at several privately owned lots on either side of Duval St.; watch for the lot attendants holding cardboard signs. You might also consider one of the convenient parking facilities described below.

Getting Around
On Foot

Strolling Key West is a great way to work off the pounds you'll be packing on by grazing the tempting kiosks, juice bars, ice-cream shops, restaurants, and, of course, bars of Key West. The sidewalk-lined streets in Old Town often front little-known lanes where unusual shops or galleries hide beneath ancient foliage. You'll miss these—and much of the mystery and charm of this southernmost city—if you don't get out of your car and walk a bit. You can explore on your own or take advantage of one of the many guided tours that are available (see our Attractions chapter for options).

On Moped or Bicycle

Key West is the perfect place to explore by moped and lends itself to bike riding with its quaint neighborhoods, alluring side streets, and lack of parking spaces., although we wouldn't recommend riding in the Mallory Square/lower Duval St. area or along North Roosevelt Blvd., which are heavily congested with people, automobiles, and delivery trucks. Many places rent a choice of either mopeds or bicycles by the hour, day, overnight, or week. Some rental choices: **Adventure Scooter & Bicycle Rentals,** 2900 North Roosevelt Blvd. (and five other locations), (305) 293-9933; **The Bicycle Center,** 523 Truman Ave., (305) 294-4556; **Bike Shop,** 1110 Truman Ave. (305) 294-1073; **Bone Island Cycle,** 1910 North Roosevelt Blvd, (305) 293-9877; **Eaton Bikes,** 830 Eaton St., (305) 294-8188; **Island Bicycles & Skateboards,** 929 Truman Ave., (305) 292-9707; **Moped Hospital,** 601 Truman

Ave., (305) 296-3344; **Paradise Rentals,** 105 Whitehead St., (305) 292-6441; **Randall J's Scooter Rentals,** 505 Greene St. (and five other locations), (305) 296-0208; and **Tropical Bicycle Rentals,** 1300 Duval St., (305) 294-8136.

> **i** **Another option on the self-propelled transportation scene is Electric Cars of Key West (100 Grinnell St.; 305-294-0995). These egg-shaped electric vehicles are eerily quiet and understandably slow. They seat two or four, have no doors, and top out at 25 mph, making them ideal for an island where the speed limits never go above 35.**

Public Transportation
By Bus

Public transport city buses, many of which are brightly decorated with the works of local artists, circle the island of Key West several times a day along color-coded routes Signs at all of the bus stops sport colored dots to indicate the routes they serve. Remember that this is an island where the buses traverse in a great big circle. You simply cannot get lost if you stay on a particular bus since it will eventually return to the stop where you boarded it. For more information call the **Key West Department of Transportation (KWDOT)** for directions (627 Palm Ave.; 305-292-8160;

www.keywestcity.com). At press time the fare was $1.00 for adults, free for children younger than age five, and .50 cents for seniors (but seniors must first obtain a senior identification card for $2 at the KWDOT office). The bus drivers do not carry change, so you must have exact fare.

> **i** **Take a tour of Key West the slow-and-easy way in a velotaxi, better known as a pedicab (Paradise Pedicab; 401 Southard St.; 305-292-0077). These bicycle-powered vehicles are a great way to feel the warm breeze on your face and breathe in the tropical air as your cyclist narrates the sights. A most unique mode of transportation in this most unique town.**

By Trolley

Listen to a narrative of historic Key West on this continuous loop **Trolley Tour** (Old Town Trolley Tours of Key West; Key West Welcome Center; 3840 North Roosevelt Blvd.; 305-395-4958, 800-213-2474; www.historictours.com). Although this transportation option is promoted and sold as a 90-minute tour, you can hop on and off the trolley as many times per day as you wish. It's one hassle-free way to shop, dine, or take in the myriad attractions Key West has to offer. Parking is free at the Key West Welcome Center, where you can also buy tickets and board the trolley. Day-trippers will find the welcome center readily accessible upon entry into Key West.

By Taxi

Try **Airport Cab Company** (305-292-1111), **Five 6's Cab Company** (305-296-6666, www.keywesttaxi.com), or **Friendly Cab Company** (305-295-5555).

> **i** An infamous bumper sticker seen frequently in the Keys is SLOW DOWN, THIS AIN'T THE MAINLAND. Slow and easy is the way most of the locals like, and that mindset is part of the required daily dose of living in paradise.

Accommodations

Selections here are mostly based on attributes of rooms, service, location, and overall ambience. For additional listings of B&Bs and guesthouse, see the PopOut maps.

Price Code Key

This key is based on high-season room rates for double occupancy without additional fees and without the 11.5 percent room tax.

$	$100 and less
$$	$100–$150
$$$	$151–$250
$$$$	$251 and above

Beachside Resort and Conference Center $$$$
3841 North Roosevelt Blvd.
(305) 296-8100, (800) 546-0885
www.beachsidekeywest.com

Proudly standing sentinel at the entrance to Key West on Roosevelt Blvd., on the banks of the Gulf of Mexico, you will discover the newest resort to open in this southernmost city. With no expenses spared, this up-scale property is impressive. There are 222 rooms, all dressed up in designer furniture, flat screen TVs, and marble to marvel you, everywhere! Elegance abounds here, but still with a Key West charm about the property. There is a heated pool on the grounds.

Casa Marina Resort and Beach Club $$$$
1500 Reynolds St.
(305) 296-3535, (866) 397-6342
www.casamarinaresort.com

The grand dame of hotels, construction of the hotel dates back to 1918, after railroad magnate Henry Flagler envisioned a resort for wealthy snowbirds. The beautiful property is a Florida Keys fairy tale, a legend that has hosted the likes of baseball great Lou Gehrig, movie star Rita Hayworth, and President Harry Truman. Casa Marina offers timeless, tasteful luxury in all of their 311 guest rooms and 72 suites.

Crowne Plaza Key West La Concha $$–$$$$
430 Duval St.
(305) 296-2991, (800) 745-2191
www.laconchakeywest.com

If you truly want to stay where the action is, you can't do better than this. Not only is La Concha the tallest building on the island of Key West, but it's also situated smack-dab in the center of the busy Duval St. scene. Today its 150 guest rooms and 10 suites have a casual yet elegant feel. The spacious pool, set amid lush island foliage, features a multilevel sundeck and tiki bar serving snacks and tropical libations. The seventh-floor wraparound deck offers a bird's-eye perspective on downtown Key West and is

one of the best places in town to view the sunset.

Hyatt Key West Resort & Spa $$$–$$$$
601 Front St.
(305) 809-1234, (888) 591-1234
www.hyatt.com

Fronting on the Gulf of Mexico, the five-story Hyatt Key West is a three-building, 118-unit complex of standard rooms and suites, all with sliding glass doors and private balconies. Rooms overlook the city, pool, or Gulf of Mexico. Hyatt has an outdoor swimming pool and hot tub, two restaurants, a small health club, two dive boats, a charter fishing boat, and a 68-foot sailing yacht for afternoon snorkeling and early-evening sunset sails.

The Inn at Key West $$$
3420 North Roosevelt Blvd.
(305) 294-5541, (800) 330-5541
www.theinnatkeywest.com

Dazzling landscaping and interior decorating, The Inn is conveniently located just 3 miles from Duval St. With 105 rooms, this complex can accommodate a getaway for two or a family reunion for 20. All rooms are decorated in Tommy Bahama furnishings. On premises is the largest tropical freshwater pool in Key West.

Ocean Key Resort and Spa $$$–$$$$
Zero Duval St.
(305) 296-7701, (800) 328-9815
www.oceankey.com

A large resort with an intimate flavor. Among the 100 units in this five-story resort are guest rooms and one- and two-bedroom, two-bath suites furnished with laminated wood and other lightweight furnishings. A highlight of Ocean Key Resort is its sunset pier overlooking both the harbor and Mallory Square. The tranquil Spa Terra, a 2,550-square-foot Indonesian-inspired spa, is a serene escape.

Pier House Resort and Caribbean Spa $$$–$$$$
1 Duval St.
(305) 296-4600, (800) 723-2791
www.pierhouse.com

The Pier House offers 126 luxurious, tropically appointed standard rooms. Lush tropical foliage and brick paving surround the swimming pool and outdoor hot tub. The resort's private beach and a secluded island glisten in the distance. The hotel is noted for its full-service spa, which offers fitness facilities, facials, massages, and hair and nail care.

The Reach Resort $$$–$$$$
1435 Simonton St.
(305) 296-5000, (866) 397-6427
www.reachresort.com

Splendor by the sea, the resort boasts the only natural sand beach on the island of Key West. All 226 guest rooms and suites are furnished with sunny lemon-colored walls, terra cotta tiled floors, with Caribbean artistic touches and private balconies. The resort has an outdoor swimming pool, hot tub, and full water-sports concession for rafts, parasailing, personal watercraft rentals, and more.

Southernmost Hotel $–$$$
1319 Duval St.
(305) 296-5611, (800) 354-4455
www.southernmostresorts.com

Gingerbread architectural detail and native flora all come together here. Southernmost Hotel's six buildings are trimmed with exotic plants, flowers, and trees. The 127 guest rooms have either two double beds or a king- or queen-size bed; some rooms include sleeper sofas. One of the hotel's two swimming pools sits in the center of the parking lot, concealed by lush greenery and a wall.

Southernmost on the Beach $–$$$$
508 South St.
(305) 296-6577, (800) 354-4455
www.southernmostresorts.com

So you want to stay right on the beach? At a gorgeous new property? This 80 room lodging will pamper you and your party. Suites are 400 sq. feet with 13 oceanfront and 48 with ocean views. On site is a private pier and pool with bar. Duval St. is just a block away but once on this lovely new resort, you will think you are on a deserted island.

Sunset Key Guest Cottages $$$-$$$$
245 Front St.
(305) 292-5300, (888) 477-7786
www.sunsetkeyisland.com

Billed as the ultimate island hideaway, the guest cottages at Sunset Key are an extension of the Key West Hilton Resort and Marina, tucked away directly across the harbor from the main hotel, overlooking Mallory Square. Access is strictly by private launch, which operates 24 hours a day between Sunset Key and the Hilton marina. The cottages offer an opportunity to truly get away from the hustle and bustle of Duval St., yet still enjoy the heart of Key West. In addition to a white-sand beach, the island features a freshwater pool, hot tub, two tennis courts, and a health club.

The Westin Key West Resort and Marina $$$-$$$$
245 Front St.
(305) 294-4000, (866) 837-4250
www.westinkeywestresort.com

The bayfront Westin was designed so all rooms (178 of them) provide views of the pool, the bay, or the marina and its surrounding waters. Guests here also are provided launch service to a relatively secluded beach at Sunset Key. On-premises are a swimming pool, hot tub, and sundeck area, fitness facilities.

Restaurants

Take in the glorious sights in the Florida Keys and then treat your taste buds to a culinary holiday. The Florida Keys yields a bounty that easily could qualify as the eighth wonder of the world. We confidently can boast that you'd be hard-pressed to find fresher, more innovatively prepared fish and seafood than in our restaurants. We import a few raw materials in the feather and flesh categories as well, so your palate will be truly well rounded. The atmosphere of our restaurants is relaxed—where even the most upscale dining carries a laid-back apparel code. You need dress no more formally than "Keys casual" (typically a tasteful ensemble of shirt and shorts, shoes, or sandals). Men may leave their sport jackets at home, and don't even think about bringing a suit to the Keys unless it is the swimming variety.

Price Code Key

Our price-code rating reflects the cost of dinner entrees for two (without cocktails, appetizers, wine, dessert, tax, or tip).

$	**Less than $25**
$$	**$25 to $40**
$$$	**$41 to $60**
$$$$	**More than $60**

Key West Classics

A&B Lobster House $$

700 Front St.
(305) 294-5880

A Key West institution among seafood connoisseurs. Situated beside the water at the foot of Front St., A&B offers a sumptuous selection of seafood and terrific views of the yachts moored in the Seaport. In addition to Maine and Florida lobster, the classic menu includes traditional oyster and clam stews, and pan roasts of slow-roasted oysters, clams, mussels, and lobsters in a broth of fresh herbs and vegetables. Steaks and pasta dishes are also available.

Alonzo's Oyster Bar $–$$

700 Front St. (downstairs)
(305) 294-5880

If you like oysters, Alonzo's is the place to go. You can order them up raw, on the half shell, baked, or batter dipped and fried. This casual eatery also serves freshly shucked clams, lobster, conch, mussels, and a variety of dishes made with the native shrimp known as "Key West pinks." If you're in the mood for a seafood soup besides chowder, try a bowl of the white clam chili. It's plenty filling but not as rich as its creamier cousin.

Blue Heaven $$
729 Thomas St.
(305) 296-8666
www.blueheavenkw.com

Blue Heaven's venue has at various times been a bordello, a pool hall, a railroad water tower, a cockfighting arena, a boxing ring, and an ice-cream parlor. Now it's a popular restaurant offering Caribbean and vegetarian cuisine in an unhampered island setting. The ambience is as legendary as its cuisine—roosters, hens, and chicks strut all around the picnic tables that fill Blue Heaven's backyard; so do the resident kitties. Jimmy Buffett's 1995 song "Blue Heaven Rendezvous" was inspired by this diamond in the rough. Patrons enjoy specialties such as jerk chicken, Caribbean shrimp, and locally caught seafood entrees. Sunday brunch at Blue Heaven draws crowds that line themselves up 'round the corner.

B.O.'s Fish Wagon $
801 Caroline St.
(305) 294-9272

No one can make you a fish sandwich like Buddy Owen. He starts with Cuban bread, then piles the fresh fish and grilled onions so high, we dare you to try to get your mouth around it. Belly up to the counter and place your order for grilled (yellowtail) or fried (grouper); add sides like fries or onion rings only if you're really hungry. The portions are huge. The menu also features squid rings (what every other restaurant in town politely calls calamari), fish-and-chips, the ubiquitous conch fritters, burgers, and hot dogs. Closed on Sunday.

Camille's Restaurant $–$$
1202 Simonton St.
(305) 296-4811
www.camilleskeywest.com

The motto is "Exotic family cooking with no boundaries," and Camille's means it. The reasonably priced menu at this eclectic local favorite features a wide array of gourmet breakfast, lunch, and dinner specials like stone-crab clawmeat cakes and Paradise Pasta—Key West pink shrimp, lobster, asparagus, and red and yellow peppers in a garlic Alfredo sauce. Weekend breakfast at

Camille's is a particular treat, offering pecan waffles, an orgy of eggs: Benedict, scrambled, whatever. And for lunch, the hand-pulled chicken salad sandwich is always a delicious choice.

Conch Republic Seafood Company $$
631 Greene St.
(305) 294-4403
www.conchrepublicseafood.com

As you've no doubt surmised, the menu here is heavy on seafood. Entrees include grilled or fried Key West pinks (shrimp), grilled tuna steak, Bahamian-style cracked conch, and pan-seared grouper fillet. For starters, try a bowl of callaloo soup—a blend of island greens and crabmeat in a spicy lobster stock. The full-service, 80-seat bar boasts one of the best rum selections around—more than 80 varieties are available.

> **i** If you like to choose a restaurant by its bill of fare, grab a copy of *The Menu*. This quarterly restaurant guide, published by the *Key West Citizen*, features menus from more than 60 Key West eateries. You'll find free copies at hotels, attractions, grocery stores, and newsstands all around Key West.

Guy Harvey's Island Grill $$
511 Greene St.
(305) 295-0019
www.guyharveyinc.com

Seafood is the signature dish here, with blue water crabs, oysters, and shrimp rounding it out. They offer sandwiches, burgers, and prime rib. One of their most popular eats is the cheesy garlic bread!

Half Shell Raw Bar $$
231 Margaret St.
(305) 294-7496
www.halfshellrawbar.com

The Half Shell Raw Bar is inches from the water and beyond casual. The focal point of the restaurant is Shucker's station, where mountains of oysters, clams, shrimp, and stone crabs are simply prepared, reasonably priced, and served with plastic utensils on paper plates at picnic tables. Half Shell carries stone crabs in season and Maine lobster. Its full bar offers beer, wine, and frozen drinks.

Harpoon Harry's $
832 Caroline St.
(305) 294-8744

Harpooned and hanging from the ceilings of this hometown-style diner is everything—including the kitchen sink. Seriously. The decor combines Tiffany light fixtures with old roller skates, sleds, carousel horses, and movie-star memorabilia. Serving luncheon and breakfast, the menu at Harpoon Harry's is much less eccentric than the decor: meat loaf or roast turkey with mashed potatoes, breaded veal cutlets, homemade chicken potpie, and melt-in-your-mouth roast pork chops with gravy. Breakfast is highlighted by Harry's Special: eggs, sausage, bacon, ham, and toast and jelly served with home fries or grits.

Hog's Breath Saloon $
400 Front St.
(305) 292-2032
www.hogsbreath.com

See listing description in "Nightlife and Entertainment" page 108.

Jimmy Buffett's Margaritaville Café $
500 Duval St.
(305) 292-1435
www.margaritaville.com/keywest

See listing description in "Nightlife and Entertainment" page 108.

Kelly's Caribbean Bar Grill & Brewery $$
301 Whitehead St.
(305) 293-8484
www.kellyskeywest.com

Named after actress Kelly McGillis, this Caribbean restaurant is on the site of the original Pan American World Airways offices with a display of early photographs and memorabilia of Pan Am service from Key West. Among the house specialties here are Caribbean Apple Chicken and Camarones Curaçao— grilled shrimp first marinated in coconut milk, lime juice, ginger, and teriyaki. Kelly's is also home to the Southernmost Brewery, which brews up an all-natural selection including Key West Golden Ale and Havana Red Ale.

Lobo's Grill $
5 Key Lime Square
(305) 296-5303

Lobo's is where locals love to lunch. The menu includes burgers, nachos, quesadillas, and salads. But the real standouts are the roll-up sandwiches—a mix of meats, cheeses, fresh veggies, and spreads tucked tightly, then rolled, in a giant flour tortilla. No credit cards.

Paradise Cafe $
1000 Eaton St.
(305) 296-5001

Choose from 15 lunchtime varieties—everything from ham and cheese, sliced turkey, and hot Italian beef to chicken salad, tuna salad, and barbecue pork—all made to order on Cuban bread with the fixin's you select. Paradise Cafe also serves up breakfast sandwiches. No credit cards.

Steakhouses

Commodore Waterfront Steakhouse $$$
700 Front St. at Key West Historic Seaport
(305) 294-9191

Tables covered in white linen are surrounded by mahogany paneling, brick walls, and lush greenery. The establishment offers some top-notch meat and seafood to match the refined ambience.

Signature dishes include Oysters Commodore, lightly breaded, flash-fried, and topped with remoulade and New York Steak Roquefort topped with melted Roquefort cheese.

Michaels $$$
532 Margaret St.
(305) 295-1300
www.michaelskeywest.com

Owners Michael Wilson (along with his wife Wilson) was the former corporate chef for Morton's Steakhouses. His prime beef is flown in fresh from Allen Brothers in Chicago. The Filet al Forno, rubbed with roasted garlic and Roquefort, has garnered rave reviews and numerous awards. The menu also includes seafood and pasta specialties. A good selection of fondues is available in the Garden Bar. No matter which entree you select, be sure to save room for dessert. Martini drinkers will appreciate the wide selection of vodkas and olives—they're stuffed with everything from the traditional pimientos to blue cheese, anchovies, and prosciutto.

> **The restaurants in Key West are as eclectic as the culture. Even for an insider, choosing a restaurant is difficult, but if you go to www.keywestmenu.com, it will help you narrow down the delectable temptations!**

Pepe's Cafe & Steak House $$

806 Caroline St.
(305) 294-7192
www.pepescafe.net

Billed as the "Eldest Eating House in the Florida Keys, established 1909," Pepe's is as beloved to Conchs and Key Westers as the Mallory Square sunset celebration. Pepe's touts its Apalachicola Bay oysters, when available, as among its specialties: raw, baked, Florentine, Mexican, or Rudi style. Also New York strip steaks, filet mignon, pork chops, even barbecue. And Pepe's burgers sound as intriguing as they taste: White Collar Burger, Blue Collar Burger, Slit Ray Burger, and Patty Melt. Be sure to try a margarita here (the lime juice is squeezed fresh).

Prime Steakhouse $$$

951 Caroline St.
(305) 296-4000

The decor is nothing like the Technicolor offerings of other bars and restaurants in the Keys. What you notice first is the cool sensation of dark mahogany and richly upholstered booths. The tables are covered with crisp white linen cloths and tall drinking vessels. The menu is limited, but they offer local seafood and the beef steak selections are outstanding. One of the house specialties is home-fried potatoes that are mashed and then fried. A feat in itself!

Restaurants 31

Strip House $$$–$$$$
1435 Simonton St.
(305) 296-5000, (800) 447-4136
www.reachresort.com

The trend setting steakhouse features prime meats, goose fat potatoes and truffle creamed spinach. Be sure and ask for their signature 24-layer chocolate cake—highly recommended! If that is too-o-o much then do go for the Australian Homemade Ice-Cream offering.

Turtle Kraals Waterfront Seafood Grill and Bar $–$$
231 Margaret St.
(305) 294-2640
www.turtlekraals.com

See listing description in "Nightlife and Entertainment" page 114.

Island Eclectic

Bagatelle $$–$$$
115 Duval St.
(305) 296-6609
www.bagatelle-keywest.com

Bagatelle serves fresh local ingredients with island inventiveness. Try the Pecan Dolphin or the Bahamian Cracked Conch Steak (if available) for something different. Or enjoy avocado fan salad or a seafood puff pastry stuffed with the catch of the day. Wraparound balconies on both levels afford outdoor dining, or you may choose to dine indoors where the decor favors that of a first-rate art gallery.

Bistro 245 $$$
245 Front St., at the Westin Key West Resort and Marina
(305) 294-4000

Imagine, a Sunday brunch buffet table that is 70 foot long—so long you can barely see the other end! Dine indoors or out with a panoramic view of the Gulf of Mexico all the while indulging in great Florida Keys cuisine. Regular menu offerings Monday through Saturday and the enormous food fest is Sunday only.

Cafe Marquesa $$$$
600 Fleming St.
(305) 292-1919
www.cafemarquesa.com

Reminiscent of a European brasserie, this restaurant oozes style. Golden walls covered with paintings, pastel tile floors, large mirrors, and a panoramic country-kitchen mural set the scene for one of the finest dining encounters in Key West. Specialties of the house have included Peppercorn Dusted Seared Yellowfin Tuna, Feta and Pine Nut Encrusted Rack of Lamb, and Grilled, Marinated Key West Shrimp.

Harbour View Café
1 Duval St., Located in the Pier House Resort
(305) 296-4600
www.pierhouse.com

Rendering of a classic setting that is well worth the price of a dinner tab. Located in the Pier House Resort (see Accommodations chapter) the menu is full-blown

"Floribbean" with all the trimmings. Get your taste buds in gear with curry chicken salad with grapes and almonds or shrimp and papaya. The white conch chowder will make you melt right into your entrée of seafood pasta, lobster or sea scallops. Reservations are a must for this popular dinner spot while in Key West.

Hot Tin Roof $$$
Zero Duval St. at Ocean Key Resort
(305) 296-7701, (800) 328-9815
www.oceankey.com

The Hot Tin Roof name comes from Tennessee Williams's (a past resident of Key West) most famous play, *Cat on a Hot Tin Roof*. The dining room and outdoor deck enjoy panoramic views of Key West Harbor and its famed sunset. The chef has combined elements of South American, Asian, and French cuisine in an interpretation of flavors and attitudes of Key West he calls "Conch-fusion." Prime examples of this gustatory philosophy include Seafood Paella with Lobster, and an ahi tuna ceviche appetizer. The Stage Door Lounge serves themed signature cocktails and offers live jazz music some evenings.

Latitudes Beach Cafe $$$
Sunset Key
(305) 294-4000
www.westinkeywestresort.com

Just five minutes across the water on Sunset Key (a private island, half of which is devoted to guest cottages, the other to pricey waterfront homes). Latitudes might just as well be half a world away. Granted, it takes some planning to get here. You have to make a reservation, and you have to board a boat. The cuisine is best described as eclectic. Dinner entrees include the likes of Pan-seared Chilean Sea Bass, Coconut-and-macadamia-encrusted Grouper, Key Lime Chicken Piccata, and Beef Tenderloin with Gorgonzola-scallion butter and a marinated portobello mushroom. A full bar offers exotic frozen island drinks as well as beer and wine.

Louie's Backyard $$$$
700 Waddell Ave.
(305) 294-1061
www.louiesbackyard.com

An enduring favorite among locals and visitors alike, Louie's Backyard combines island manor house ambience with cutting-edge cuisine. A sweeping veranda, for outdoor dining, overlooks Louie's "backyard," which is actually a prime piece of Atlantic oceanfront property. In the '70s this spot was a favorite with next-door-neighbor Jimmy Buffett, who often played for his supper. Dinner entrees span the globe, with fresh local seafood garnering center stage. Sample dinner offerings include sautéed Key West shrimp with bacon, mushrooms, and stone-ground grits or sautéed grouper with Asian vegetables, or grilled veal chop with stewed sweet onions and mustard seeds. An equally innovative

cuisine is offered on the lunch menu for nearly half the price of evening dining.

Nicola Seafood $$$
601 Front St.
At the Hyatt Key West Resort and Spa
(305) 296-9900
www.keywest.hyatt.com

Located at the corner of Simonton and Front streets at the Hyatt Key West Resort and Marina, Nicola specializes in island fare—fresh fish and seafood blackened, grilled, or sautéed and served with a sauce on the side. Popular dishes include Sweet Potato Pecan Crusted Yellowtail, topped with rum-basted bananas; Moroccan Rubbed Sea Bass with cucumber-yogurt slaw and Israeli couscous; and the appetizer Wild Mushroom Crespelle, which is a crepe stuffed with Boursin cheese and wild mushrooms, draped in Chardonnay sauce.

nine one five $$
915 Duval St.
(305) 296-0669
www.915duval.com

Snappy concept with gastronomical success! The chefs at nine one five have created dishes meant to mix and match and be served with wine. Upscale without being pretentious and loaded with atmosphere, this restaurant, housed in a stately Victorian home, is the talk of the town. While you're waiting for your meal, try an appetizer like tuna dome made with Dungeness crab and diced

Granny Smith apples in lemon miso, wrapped with sushi-grade Ahi tuna. Don't miss the seared sea scallops with black truffle butter and sautéed rapini. And for dessert, how about Earl Grey crème brûlée?

Rooftop Cafe $$$
310 Front St.
(305) 294-2042

High amid the treetops, Rooftop Cafe looks down on the tourist mecca along Front St. near Mallory Square. And although the restaurant bustles with dining activity, the atmosphere remains unhurried and removed from the fray. The cuisine, innovative in both composition and presentation, combines local piscatory resources with an international flair. Dinner creations have included Sautéed Pepper Tiger Tuna, a tuna steak with black pepper and sesame seeds served with soy-wasabi sauce and mung sprouts and Shellfish Lasagna, a chef's selection of seafood under a blanket of lemon-pepper pasta served on a lobster and oregano coulis.

Seven Fish $$
632 Olivia St.
(305) 296-2777
www.7fish.com

The environment at Seven Fish is cozy and friendly and the food flavorful and inexpensive. In addition to fresh fish, the menu includes grilled chicken, meat loaf, New York strip steak, and a variety of salad choices. Seven Fish is small—go early or you may have to wait—and the tables are quite close together.

Square One $$$
1075 Duval St.
(305) 296-4300
www.squareonerestaurant.com

Enjoy a touch of class and a bit of craziness, Manhattan style, at Square One, a casually sophisticated uptown bistro in Duval Square. Two enormous tropical floral murals flank the walls, offsetting the highly polished wood decor. Diners are treated to light piano music as they try these signature dishes: roast rack of lamb encrusted with Pommery mustard and served with honey shallot confit and minted bordelaise sauce, or sautéed sea scallops served on a bed of poached spinach with a light champagne mustard-cream sauce. And there is always a chef's choice pasta selection and other daily specialties.

Melting Pot

Ambrosia Japanese Restaurant $$
1401 Simonton St.
(305) 293-0304

The sun rises brightly on this wildly favorite Japanese restaurant. With a panoply of sushi, sakes and good services, the diverse flavors and textures combined with outstanding sauces, will beckon you for a return engagement.

Antonia's Restaurant $$

615 Duval St.
(305) 294-6565
www.antoniaskeywest.com

Elegant, yet understated, Antonia's is a great place to go if you want to dress up. The menu changes every evening, but virtually all the restaurant's veal dishes are popular and past offerings have included grilled filet of beef tenderloin, served with mushrooms, brandy, and cream; pan-seared yellowtail braised with watercress, endive, radicchio, and white wine; and Linguine Cousteau, a variety of shellfish served in a fresh tomato sauce.

Azur $$$

425 Grinnell St.
(305) 292-2987
Mediterranean

Toss Greek, Italian, and Iberian cuisines in with a tropical setting and you get a creation of a Mediterranean mix called Azur. The pride of Azur is the local fresh fish and other catch flown in from Hawaii or Greece (served within 24 hours). Sunday brunch is not to be missed and showcases creative dishes such as crab or prime rib benedicts and angel hair pasta carbonara with poached eggs.

Banana Cafe $$$
1215 Duval St.
(305) 294-7227

Settle into this quiet open-air French bistro, and choose from more than 40 breakfast and lunch crepes. The exterior of Banana Cafe resembles a quaint Caribbean cottage; the airy interior says French bistro, with pinkish pine wood, artistic black-and-white photography, ceiling fans, and a small piano bar. Dining also is offered on the front balcony or along the side on a wood deck shaded by large tropical trees.

The Continent Abbondanza $
1208 Simonton St.
(305) 292-1199

At last, a place to enjoy casual Italian fare in Old Town. The specialty here is pasta, of course, in a variety of shapes and with sauces that range from marinara to Alfredo. You'll also find such main dishes as chicken Marsala and veal Parmesan, plus daily specials.

El Meson de Pepe $$
410 Wall St.
(305) 295-2620
www.elmesondepepe.com

Situated just off Mallory Square, this Cuban favorite draws a large post-sunset crowd. A salsa band plays nightly as the sun sinks into the Gulf of Mexico, which adds to the festive and welcoming atmosphere. Look for

Cuban-Conch classics on the menu—Mollete a la Pancho; Cuban bread stuffed with picadillo, a spicy combination of ground beef, capers, raisins, olives, and seasonings; and ropa vieja. Quench your thirst with a mojito.

El Siboney $
900 Catherine St.
(305) 296-4184

A cascade of bilingual chatter washes over the enthusiastic diners at El Siboney restaurant, an informal restaurant specializing in Cuban cuisine. Hot, buttery Cuban bread is immediately whisked to your table, and then begins the difficult decision of which taste-tempting delicacy to order. Portions are enormous at El Siboney and we recommend one of the combination platters: A platter of roast pork, black beans, yellow rice, and cassava is served heaped with raw onions. Crab, shrimp, and chicken all get the wonderful Cuban garlic treatment, and you can choose paella for two persons. No credit cards.

Finnegan's Wake Irish Pub & Eatery $
320 Grinnell St.
(305) 293-0222
www.keywestirish.com

See listing description in "Nightlife and Entertainment" page 106.

The Grand Café $$$
314 Duval St.
(305) 292-4740
www.grandcafekeywest.com

Southern French cuisine of Provence. The owners and chef demand nothing short of the best from themselves and the food is consequently at the same level. The sauces are light and represent the flavors of southern French cooking, with fresh herbs and olive oil. Excellent wine selections and simply grand martinis. *C'est bon.*

Jose's Cantina $
800 White St.
(305) 296-4366

Step inside this little neighborhood diner and you might believe you'd just walked in from the streets of Havana. The owners are Cuban, and so are most of the customers. But even if you don't speak Spanish, you're sure to receive a hearty *bienvenida* (welcome) here. The menus are in English, the waitstaff is bilingual, and the food is plentiful, delicious, and cheap. Jose's has one of the best Cuban mixes on the island—that's a sandwich combination of ham and shredded pork on Cuban bread with lettuce, tomato, mayo, mustard, onions, and pickles. The dinners—Cuban variations on chicken, pork, and beef—come with the traditional black beans, yellow rice, and plantains.

Kyushu Japanese Restaurant $$
921 Truman Ave.
(305) 294-2995

Take off your shoes! Kyushu provides an authentic Japanese dining experience in tatami rooms, or individual low-to-the-ground tables and benches secluded by bamboo screens. The menu includes an extensive selection of sushi—including eel, conch, octopus, yellowtail, tuna, and snapper.

La Trattoria $$
524 Duval St.
(305) 296-1075

This upscale SoHo–style New York bistro rates as a Key West treasure. A romantic taste of old Italy favored by locals, visitors, and Keys residents from as far away as Key Largo, La Trattoria redefines the traditional pasta, veal, chicken, lamb, and seafood dishes of the mother country. The sophisticated decor belies the fact that you are a stone's throw from the sidewalks of busy Duval St. Try Agnello alla Griglia (lamb with fresh rosemary) or Cheese Tortellina alla Romana, with smoked ham and peas in a parmigiana cream sauce.

Mangia Mangia $$
900 Southard St.
(305) 294-2469
www.mangia-mangia.com

Off the main drag but definitely on the right track is this pasta lovers' nirvana. Mangia Mangia ("eat, eat") bestows a passel of homemade fresh pasta and finely seasoned sauces that would excite any palate. The chefs work their macaroni magic in plain view. You can always order the basic sauces—marinara, Alfredo, pesto, meat, and red or white seafood—but for something out of the ordinary, try Bollito Misto di Mare—fresh scallops, shrimp, conch, salmon, and local fish in a garlicky clam sauce.

Martin's Cafe Restaurant $$
917 Duval St.
(305) 296-0111

Achtung! Achtung! Martin's expansive German menu with its island flair now shines bright on upper Duval St. You'll find classic German dishes such as pepper steak, sauerbraten with spaetzle and red cabbage, and Wiener schnitzel, but Martin's also prepares island seafood creations a la deutsch. Grouper Dijon and Sea Scallops Wunderbar (baked with spinach encased in puff pastry).

Origami Japanese Restaurant $$
1075 Duval St.
(305) 294-0092

The stark white decor of Origami provides a backdrop for the brightly colored tropical fish adorning the walls. And like the Japanese art of folding paper into decorative or representational forms—origami—the restaurant fashions fresh, local seafood into exquisite sushi and sashimi.

Pisces $$$$
1007 Simonton St.
(305) 294-7100
www.pisceskeywest.com

This enduring tropical French establishment has won awards and accolades from *Gourmet, Bon Appétit,* and *Wine*

Spectator magazines, and the recognition is well deserved. At Pisces, creativity culminates in such delicacies as Lobster Tango Mango and Raspberry Duck. One of its finest treasures is Yellowtail Atocha, snapper sautéed in tarragon butter with shrimp and scallops. Specials are available nightly.

Santiago's Bodega $$
207 Petronia St.
(305) 296-7691

Tucked away on a small street with a neighborhood setting, you discover Santiago's Bodega. Wood floors, warm colors, and wide, open windows pouring out onto a porch for dining under gossamer lanterns capture the setting for this unique tapas experience. The food is fresh and simple with more than 30 selections on the menu including soups and salads. Shrimp with ginger and lemongrass, grilled chicken with secret spice, and yellowfish ceviche are on the offering. Loads of vegetarian dishes but not 100 percent vegan. Wine, beer, lovely sherry, and ports are also served. Service is charming and friendly. Open for lunch and dinner, but be mindful to make reservations—everyone wants a table!

Sarabeth's $$
530 Simonton St.
(305) 293-8181
www.sarabeths.com

There is a real Sarabeth, and she is an award-winning jam maker, pastry chef, and restaurateur. Her "empire" include four locations in New York City and now Key West. The James Beard award-winning menus include from-scratch pancakes, salads, sandwiches, meat loaf, grilled meats, and fish. The coffee is served in cups so large they are called bowls. When you partake of any item, you are made to feel as though you are sitting in Sarabeth's personal kitchen where everything is created just for you.

One of a Kind

Better Than Sex Dessert Café
411 Petronia St.
(305) 393-1049

This romantic place will put you in the mood . . . for dessert.

Blond Giraffe
1209 Truman Ave., (305) 293-6667
and 629 Duval St., (305) 293-6998
www.blondgiraffe.com

Key lime pie . . . mmmm.

The Café
509 Southard St.
(305) 296-5515

Truly vegetarian and vegan but in no way dull and bland.

The Coffee and Tea House of Key West
1211 Duval St.
(305) 295-0788

Sit a spell and watch the world go by.

Coffee Plantation
713 Caroline St.
(305) 295-9808
www.coffeeplantationkeywest.com

Enjoy a delicious coffee, tea, smoothies, or frappes and check your e-mail on one of the computers here.

Cole's Peace Artisan Bakery
1111 Eaton St.
(305) 292-0703
www.colespeace.com

Famous Cuban and mango breads, Mexican chocolate cake, and ciabatta lotta sandwiches.

Croissants de France
816 Duval St.
(305) 294-2624

This beloved, tiny treasure also dishes up galettes, quiches, croissants, and brioche sandwiches. Oooo la la!

Damn Good Food To-Go
700 Front St.
(305) 294-0011

This always-open, never-closed, eat-in, take-it-out, have-it-come-to-you emporium has everything you need to appease your late-night munchies.

Dennis Island Cafe
316 Petronia St.
(305) 294-1577

Quaint cafe tables holding plates of famous Dennis selections including Cuban, Conch, and American comfort food makes this eatery feel like home.

Fausto's Food Palace
522 Fleming St., (305) 296-5663
and 1105 White St., (305) 294-5221
www.faustos.com

"Not just a grocery, a social center" reads the slogan in the ads for this gourmet food emporium, which has been serving Key West since 1926. Here, in addition to the usual grocery staples are fresh local seafood, premium meats and poultry, caviar, pâtés, rare cheeses, desserts, and more than 700 varieties of wine.

5 Brothers
930 Southard St.
(305) 296-5205

This is where Key West goes for buche, that tiny cup of industrial-strength Cuban coffee that satisfies your caffeine habit with a single swig and gets your juices flowing. This tiny corner grocery also makes a mean Cuban mix—that's a combination ham/pork/salami/Swiss/lettuce/pickle sandwich served on Cuban bread—and great conch chowder (Friday only).

Flamingo Crossing
1107 Duval St.
(305) 296-6124

The place to pause for refreshment as you make your way up and down Duval. Fresh homemade ice cream is the business here, and it's the closest thing to Italian gelato this side of the Mediterranean. If you're just in the mood for a thirst-quencher, try a key limeade.

Kermit's Key West Key Lime Shoppe
200 Elizabeth St.
(305) 296-0806
www.keylimeshop.com

You can't miss this place because the key lime chef is outside waving you in to key lime heaven. Everything inside is made with key lime juice, including oils, cookies, candy kisses, salad dressings, juice concentrate, pie filling, and sweets of all sorts.

Key West Key Lime Pie Company
701 Caroline St.
(305) 294-6567

Each handmade, 9-inch pie (also sold by the slice) is frozen, literally melting in your mouth, bite by bite. If a fork isn't your style, how about key lime pie on a stick, dipped in dark chocolate? Messy to eat, but, oh, so yummy.

Key West Tea & Coffee
608 Front St.
(305) 292-7998, (888) 840-1280
www.keywesttea.com

Serving many infusion teas (the sun-glow tea made with apple, hibiscus, rosehips, papaya, pineapple, and orange, is a favorite) and excellent coffee.

Mam's Best Food
405 Petronia St.
(305) 292-3855

Mam's is a tiny Kosher shop with a huge following. Some local grocery stores in Key West carry limited kosher, but not enough to fulfill the tourist and local requirements like Mam's can. The owner makes a bi-monthly trip to Miami to buy top-quality kosher meats.

Mattheessen's 4th of July Ice Cream Parlor
1110 White St.
(305) 294-8089

The original 4th of July Restaurant opened its doors in the 1950s and this Key West tradition has been revived by the Mattheessen family, who remodeled the old eatery with red, white, and blue décor and are now offer ice cream, marble-slab fudge, cookies, and barbecue to old aficionados and enthusiastic newcomers.

Peppers of Key West
602 Greene St.
(305) 295-9333, (800) 597-2823
www.peppersofkeywest.com

Chile peppers are the name of the game here (which bills itself as "the hottest spot on the island"). More than 300 varieties of hot sauces grace the shelve. Peppers always has a basket of chips and a few open bottles at the front counter so you can have a taste, if you dare.

Salute
1000 Atlantic Blvd.
(305) 292-1117

This locals hang out is a pet of a restaurant for all of us in the know. Yummy seafood, great Italian choices with the antipasto winning hands down.

Sandy's Cafe
1026 White St.
(305) 295-0159

This hole-in-the-wall Cuban walk-up joint is one of the best places in the Keys for authentic Cuban "fast food." The lines outside the order windows (no seating available) indicate how loyal Sandy's customers are. The cafe con leche, cheese tostada, and Cuban mix sandwiches will have you clamoring for more. Cash and carry only.

Sugar Apple Natural Foods
917 Simonton St.
(305) 292-0043

A longtime favorite of health-conscious Key Westers, Sugar Apple stocks organic and hard-to-find groceries, vitamins, beauty aids, homeopathic remedies, books, and herbs. A juice bar and deli serve up sandwiches, smoothies, specials, and teas.

Attractions

Put on your sandals, grab your hat—there is lots to see and do in Key West. Don't wait for a rainy day to explore our historical sites, museums, nature preserves, and marine research centers—you might not have one!

Historic Homes and Museums

**Audubon House &
Tropical Gardens**
205 Whitehead St.
(305) 294-2116
www.audubonhouse.com

Legend has it that Audubon sketched the white-crowned pigeon and the geiger tree he found in the garden here. During his stay in the Keys, Audubon produced 18 sketches of native wildlife. Original lithographs of these drawings are on display here. The house and environs, however, are more reminiscent of the family of Capt. John Geiger, a wrecker who built the house and lived here with his family. Set your own tour pace with a free pair of headphones and a tape that brings the house alive. Audubon House is open daily. Children younger than age six are free.

Curry Mansion
511 Caroline St.
(305) 294-5349, (800) 253-3466
www.currymansion.com

This imposing home evokes images of an opulent old Key West, although the three-story Conch house now serves as the focal point for a bed-and-breakfast inn and a museum. Built in 1905 by Milton Curry, Florida's first homegrown millionaire, the inn's public rooms display a selection of antiques and memorabilia. Poke around in the attic, and you'll find an 1899 billiard table among the old dresses and luggage. From the attic you can climb the widow's walk for a panoramic view of Key West Harbor. Self-guided tours are available daily.

East Martello Museum
3501 South Roosevelt Blvd.
(305) 296-3913
www.kwahs.com

This enchanting, artifact-filled former fort will bring you up to speed on Key West history. Built during the Civil War, the brick fortress was never completely finished because the circular Martello design became antiquated before it was ever armed. Operated today as a museum and gallery by the Key West Art and Historical Society, the 8-foot-thick walls support pictures, artifacts, and historical documents. Featured in the small gallery are the charming wood carvings of Key West's Mario Sanchez and the funky welded sculptures by the late Stanley Papio of Key Largo, fabricated from bedsprings, toilet fixtures, and other so-called junk. You can climb the citadel to the lookout tower for an unobstructed view of the Atlantic coast. East Martello Museum is open daily. Kids younger than age six get in free.

> **Adults may purchase a combination ticket that allows admission to the East Martello Museum museum, the Key West Lighthouse Museum, and the Key West Museum of Art and History at the Custom House. Visits to all three facilities need not be made on the same day.**

Florida Keys Historical Military Memorial
One Mallory Square

Flush in military history, Key West honors its best with this handsome memorial dedicated to those who have proudly served their country and the military events directly affecting Key West and the Keys. Beginning in 1822, when the U.S. Navy raised the American flag over Key West, the era of the Spanish-American War, through WW I and WW II, Korea, the Cuban missile crisis, Vietnam, Desert Storm, Iraq, and the ongoing war on drugs, this simple, elegant display stands proud as a sentinel reflecting a community paying homage to these historical events and brave souls.

Harry S Truman Little White House
111 Front St.
(305) 294-9911
www.trumanlittlewhitehouse.com

Ordered by his doctor to retreat to a stress-free climate and recover from a lingering cold, President Harry S Truman came to Key West for the first time in 1946. Like so many others, he was instantly smitten with the island and spent 11 working vacations in the commandant's quarters, dubbed the Little White House. Built in 1890, the house was renovated for its famed visitor in 1948. Opened to the general public as a museum dedicated to "Give 'Em Hell Harry" in 1991, the home has once again been restored to its 1948 splendor. You'll be able to view Truman's Winter White House as it looked when he spent his 175 working vacation days here. The family quarters, poker porch, dining room, and living room (complete with Truman's piano) are open to the public. Guided tours are conducted daily. Children younger than age four are admitted free.

Hemingway Home and Museum
907 Whitehead St.
(305) 294-1136
www.hemingwayhome.com

Once the home of Key West's most famous writer, Ernest Hemingway, the Hemingway Home and Museum ranks at the top of any must-do list and is Key West's most popular attraction. Built by wrecker Asa Tift in 1851, the home took on historical significance when Ernest and Pauline Hemingway moved in. Pauline spearheaded extensive remodeling, redecorating, and refurnishing and fitted her backyard with the island's first swimming pool. Hemingway wrote several of his most celebrated works, including *For Whom the Bell Tolls*, *Death in the Afternoon*, *The Green Hills of Africa*, and *To Have and Have Not*, from his pool house office out back. The Hemingways lived in this Key West home from 1931 to 1939. Guided tours lasting approximately 45 minutes are offered every 10 minutes, daily. Children younger than age six enter free. Be sure to look for the infamous six-toed cats!

Heritage House Museum and Robert Frost Cottage
410 Caroline St.
(305) 296-3573
www.heritagehousemuseum.org

The memorabilia in the Heritage House Museum pays tribute to Jessie Porter, a cultured, well-traveled woman at the center of Key West society in the mid-1900s. Visitors to the house included Tallulah Bankhead, Thornton Wilder, Gloria Swanson, Tennessee Williams, Pauline Hemingway, and, of course, regular visitor Robert Frost, who stayed in the small cottage in the rear garden when he wintered in Key West, which he did off and on from 1945 through 1960. Visitors are invited to make themselves at home in the comfortable original surroundings and even to play the antique piano. Children younger than age 12 get in free.

Key West Lighthouse and Keeper's Quarters Museum
938 Whitehead St.
(305) 294-0012
www.kwahs.com

This 1847 structure, inland on a Key West street just across from the Hemingway Home, affords visitors a bird's-eye view of Key West from atop its 90-foot light tower (88 steps to the top). Why a lighthouse so far from the water? It was positioned here to avoid the fate of its predecessor on Whitehead Point, which toppled in a hurricane the previous year. The keeper's quarters houses maritime

memorabilia and a gift shop. The lighthouse museum is open daily for self-guided tours. Children younger than age six are free.

The Key West Museum of Art and History at the Custom House
281 Front St.
(305) 295-6616
www.kwahs.com

Even if it contained no exhibits, this lovely building just off Mallory Square, where Front and Whitehead Streets come together, would be worth a stop. With its 20-foot ceilings, arched windows, 12 fireplaces, and magnificently restored staircase, the structure itself is a work of art. Inside you will find seven galleries and a gift shop. Exhibits of artwork and historical artifacts change periodically; however, those on the second floor traditionally focus on the history of Key West. Be sure to continue up the stairs to the third floor. There are no exhibit galleries here, but the works of folk artist Mario Sanchez, which line the walls between the closed office doors, are worth the climb. There's a great view from the arched window overlooking Sunset Key and the harbor here, too. The museum is open daily. Children younger than age six enter free.

Mel Fisher Maritime Heritage Society and Museum
200 Greene St.
(305) 294-2633
www.melfisher.org

For 16 years, "today's the day" was the hope of treasure salvor Mel Fisher, who finally struck pay dirt on July 20, 1985. Finding the *Nuestra Señora de Atocha*, which Fisher estimated to be worth $400 million, ensured his legacy as treasure hunter extraordinaire. Heavy gold chains, jeweled crosses, and bars of silver and gold are among the artifacts on display at the permanent first-floor exhibit. In 2007, Mel Fishers' Treasures subcontracted a company to salvage a shipwreck site The *Santa Margarita*. Their discovery of this 1622 Spanish galleon yielded a metal box full of pearls, gold artifacts, and chains. The second-floor exhibit changes frequently—call for details. A museum shop offers a variety of pirate and nautical gifts. The museum is open daily. Children younger than age six are admitted free.

The Pirate Soul Museum
524 Front St.
(305) 292-1113
www.piratesoul.com

Old artifacts and new technologies meet at this handsome museum, which brings to life the swashbuckling legends and lore of Key West. The Pirate Soul Museum depicts the era from 1690 to 1730 with more than 500 artifacts, a re-created pirate ship (that you're invited to explore), and one of two authenticated pirate flags in the world. Go on your own treasure hunt using an interactive clue-filled logbook, listen to Blackbeard speak on piracy's golden age, or read part of the original journal of Captain Kidd's last voyage. Don't miss the 1696 Wanted poster for Henry Avery and the many other authentic items here, including ceramics, dishes, and rare cannonballs. Ahoy Mate!

San Carlos Institute
516 Duval St.
(305) 294-3887
www.institutosancarlos.org

Founded in 1871 by Cuban exiles, the San Carlos Institute was established to preserve the language and traditions of the Cuban people. Dubbed "La Casa Cuba" by legendary poet and patriot José Martí, the institute helped unite the exiled Cuban community. The current building was completed in 1924 and operated as an integrated school until the mid-1970s, when deteriorating conditions necessitated its closing. With the perseverance of the Hispanic Affairs Commission, a state agency headed by Rafael Penalver, restoration of the San Carlos was completed and the institute reopened on January 3, 1992, 100 years to the day after José Martí's first visit in the late 19th century. Today the San Carlos Institute is a museum, library, school, art gallery, theater, and conference center. The institute is open Tuesday through Sunday. Admission is free.

Wrecker's Museum
322 Duval St.
(305) 294-9502

Built in 1829, this museum is known as the "oldest house in Key West." The Conch cottage was the home to Capt. Francis B. Watlington and consists of three buildings: the main house, a kitchen house, and exhibit building. Peek into the life of a wrecking family with documents and memorabilia from the salvage trade. The Wrecker's Museum is open daily. The tours are self-guided, but a docent is always available on the premises to answer questions.

One of a Kind

African Cemetery at Higgs Beach
Atlantic Blvd.

In 1860, the slave trade brought thousands of young slaves from West Africa to the New World. Hundreds were brought to Key West to be eventually shipped back home to West Africa. Unfortunately, many died in transit and the bodies were buried in mass graves in the Higgs Beach area. In 1993, these events came to the attention of a local historical researcher and in 2007, a concrete slab was poured over the grave site and the AFRICAN CEMETERY AT HIGGS BEACH sign erected as a first step in creating a lasting memorial.

Flagler Station Over-Sea Railway Historeum
901 Caroline St.
(305) 295-3562
www.flaglerstation.net

Key West can literally trace its beginnings as a tourist destination to the vision of one man—Henry Morrison Flagler—and his Key West Extension of the Florida East Coast Railroad. Flagler made his money in oil, but he made his name by building a railroad as well as luxury hotels along the east coast of Florida from Jacksonville to Miami. In 1905, at the age of 75, Flagler proposed his most daring venture to date—he instructed his engineers to extend the Florida East Coast Railroad 130 miles out to sea to Key West. The museum, part of which is housed in an actual Florida East Coast Railroad car, celebrates Flagler's magnificent obsession. Costumed "historytellers" and video footage help re-create the day in January 1912 that the Key West Extension, also known as the Over-Sea Railway, opened to great fanfare with a frail Henry Flagler himself aboard the first train to arrive in Key West. You'll see photos and memorabilia from that momentous occasion, as well as a film titled *The Day the Train Arrived,* which includes eyewitness accounts from people who were actually there and who made the trip by rail on the Key West Extension. There's an entire display devoted to the building of the Seven

Mile Bridge, an amazing engineering feat even by today's standards, as well as photos and video recollections of the devastating hurricane of 1935 that took out the Over-Sea Railway. Open daily.

Florida Keys Eco-Discovery Center
35 East Quay Rd., Truman Waterfront, Key West
(305) 292-0311, (305) 809-4700
www.fla-keys.com/keywest/ecodiscovery

With a $6 million price tag, the 6,400-square-foot Eco-Discovery Center in Old Town is operated by the National Oceanic and Atmospheric Administration's Florida Keys National Marine Sanctuary, the National Park Service, and the U.S. Fish and Wildlife Service. Located at historic Truman waterfront, the Center's high points are a 22-minute film by David Talbot, the award-winning director of *Free Willy* fame. Talbot takes you on an exciting trip from land to under the sea. In the Eco-Discovery Center you can utilize touch-screen computers to learn more about the Keys and conservation for this part of the planet, coral reefs, Keys habitats, and a walk-through version of the Aquarius Undersea Lab. In 2008, a new 2,400-gallon coral reef aquarium exhibit opened to feature hard and soft corals to educate the public about preserving our coral reefs. Stop in on Saturday mornings when kids ages kindergarten through grade five, can attend the "Discovery Saturdays" programs. To add to the marvels of this complex, there is a "green" roof that covers the main structure—talk about being eco-friendly!

Fort Zachary Taylor State Park Historical Site

Truman Annex at Southard St.
(305) 292-6713
www.forttaylor.org

Although not fully completed until 1866, this Key West military bastion served the Union well during the Civil War, when it guarded against Confederate blockade runners. So impressive were its defenses, the fort was never attacked. It saw continuous usage by the military until the federal government deeded the structure to the state of Florida for use as a historic site. The Florida Park Service opened Fort Zachary Taylor to the public in 1985.

Today, however, much of the fort is again closed to public exploration, this time because the structure has succumbed to the ravages of time. The park service secured a $1.25 million grant, used to restore the north curtain, which is where the guns were mounted. As portions of the fort are structurally repaired, they will be reopened. At present, only the parade ground, the south curtain observation deck, and the north curtain can be toured. The museum is also closed for repairs. Exhibits have been transferred to East Martello

Museum (see the Historic Homes and Museums section) until the restoration is complete.

The surrounding park offers a beach for fishing, swimming, or snorkeling, as well as picnic areas equipped with tables and grills, outside showers, snack bar, and restroom facilities. It also offers one of the best, unobstructed views of the sunset.

Fort Zachary Taylor is open daily from 8 a.m. to sunset. Hang on to your ticket stub; you may leave the park and return at any time throughout the same day by simply showing your ticket to the booth attendant.

Joe Allen Garden Center
Atlantic Blvd. and White St.
(305) 294-3210
www.keywestgardenclub.com

Built in 1862, the West Martello Tower, like the other forts on the island, was never involved in an actual war. It was, however, used for target practice by the U.S. Navy, which accounts for its somewhat shabby condition. Today the tower is also the Joe Allen Garden Center, and the Key West Garden Club operates here. Use the self-guided tour to spot local flora, including a key lime tree, or just find an inviting spot to relax. West Martello is open Tuesday through Saturday in season. The schedule may vary; call for more information. Admission is free, but note that shirt and shoes are required.

Key West AIDS Memorial
Foot of White St. and Atlantic Blvd.

Key West has been especially hard hit by the AIDS epidemic; more than 1,000 here have died. The names of many of those victims are inscribed on this memorial, which consists of flat granite slabs embedded in the walkway approaching White St. Pier. Built with private funds and dedicated on World AIDS Day, December 1, 1997, the memorial has room for 1,500 names. At the unveiling, it contained 730. New names are engraved annually and dedicated in a ceremony that takes place each December on World AIDS Day. Members of a volunteer group—Friends of the Key West AIDS Memorial—maintain and protect this site.

Key West Aquarium
1 Whitehead St. at Mallory Square
(305) 296-2051, (800) 868-7482
www.keywestaquarium.com

Key West's oldest tourist attraction (built in 1934) and still one of the most fascinating our southernmost city has to offer, the Key West Aquarium affords you a diver's-eye view of the marine creatures of our encompassing waters. Stroll at your leisure alongside the back-lit tanks re-creating our coral reefs, but don't miss the guided tours offered four times daily, when you'll witness the feeding of the species. You'll marvel at the feeding frenzy of the sharks and sawtooths; the nurse sharks and stingrays flipping and splashing for their rations; and the tarpon, barracuda, game fish, and sea turtles recognizing the hands that feed them in the outdoor Atlantic Shores Exhibit, created to look like a mangrove lagoon. A highlight for kids is the "touch tank" just inside the front door. Here, they can reach in and grab hold of horseshoe crabs, hermit crabs, conchs, sea cucumbers, and many other creatures that populate the waters surrounding Key West. Be sure to bring your camera—you'll want to capture the expression on your child's face when the horseshoe crab in his or her hand suddenly flexes its legs The aquarium is open daily. Children age three and younger are admitted free.

The Key West Butterfly & Nature Conservatory
1316 Duval St.
(305) 296-2988, (800) 839-4647
www.keywestbutterfly.com

The Key West Butterfly & Nature Conservatory was opened in January 2003 by Sam Trophia and George Fernandez, the proprietors of the perennially popular Wings of Imagination: The Butterfly Gallery. The Conservatory celebrates the lives of butterflies around the globe. Visitors first stop at the Learning Center for a brief introductory film on the wonders of the butterflies' world before

proceeding to the Miracle of Metamorphosis exhibit. Here you can watch the actual butterfly-hatching process and observe the stages of development from egg to caterpillar to chrysalis. All the butterflies are bred in captivity on butterfly farms in North, Central, and South America, as well as Southeast Asia and Africa. When mature, the butterflies are released into a 5,000-square-foot glass-enclosed greenhouse featuring more than 3,500 tropical trees and plants. The gardens are a horticulturalist's nirvana—lush and tropical vegetation inhabited by 30 to 50 species of exotic butterflies, such as Blue Morpho and Emerald Swallowtail, and myriad birds from all over the world. A gallery displays Trophia's original butterfly designs. The Conservatory is open daily. Children younger than age four are free.

Key West City Cemetery
Bordered by Angela, Frances, and Olivia Streets, and Windsor Lane
(305) 292-8177

Built in 1847 after the horrific hurricane the year before washed out the sand sanctuary at the island's southernmost point, Key West City Cemetery, right in the center of town, adds a human element to the history of Key West. The marble monuments of the wealthy were shipped to the island; local markers were generally produced from brick or coral-based cement. Carved with symbols and prosaic sayings, such as I TOLD YOU I WAS SICK and DEVOTED FAN OF JULIO IGLESIAS, the gravestones are a living legacy for those lying beneath. Some of the tombs are "bunked," or stacked, because digging in the coral rock proved difficult and seawater percolates just under the surface.

The Historic Florida Keys Foundation makes it easy to explore the Key West City Cemetery, which was recognized by the state as a Florida Heritage Site in 2006. The organization's self-guided tour pamphlet lists graves of 42 of Key West's most prominent or notorious deceased citizens, with brief personality profiles and a translation of the meaning of the carved symbols on the gravestones. Pick up a free *Historic Key West City Cemetery Self-guided Tour* pamphlet in the Florida Room at the Monroe County Public Library, 700 Fleming St., or at the Key West Chamber of Commerce, Mallory Square.

Key West Historic Seaport and HarborWalk
201 William St., at the Key West Bight
(305) 293-8309
www.keywestseaport.com

Formerly known as Key West Bight, this once-seedy piece of prime waterfront real estate was where shrimpers, spongers, and turtle traders came to unload their daily catch, tell tall tales of the sea, quaff a few brews, and just generally hang out. With the relocation of the shrimp boats to Stock Island and the demise of sponging and turtle hunting, this area has undergone a complete metamorphosis. Tall ships still tie up here, but so do million-dollar yachts. Trendy shops, restaurants, and raw bars now line a pristine wooden boardwalk that follows the bend of the coastline here from the foot of Front St. to the foot of Margaret St. Despite gentrification, this remains a busy working marina.

Key West Historical Memorial Sculpture Garden
Mallory Square
(305) 294-4142

Located on Key West's original shoreline just behind Mallory Square, this tiny fenced-in "garden" pays homage to three dozen men and women whose lives and deeds have had tremendous impact on the southernmost city. Here you will find the stories and likenesses of such former influential citizens as wreckers Asa Tift and Capt. John Geiger; Ernest Hemingway, writer; Harry S Truman, former U.S. president; railroad magnate Henry Flagler; Sister Louise Gabriel, whose Grotto to Our Lady of Lourdes is said to have protected Key West from hurricanes for more than 75 years; and Charley Toppino, land developer. All of the bronze busts, as well as the imposing wreckers sculpture, are the works of sculptor James Mastin of Coral Gables, Florida. The sculpture garden is open daily during daylight hours.

Key West Shipwreck Historeum
1 Whitehead St., Mallory Square
(305) 292-8990

Relive the days of wreckers, lumpers, and divers at the Shipwreck Historeum—part museum, part theater—where actors, video footage, and interactive presentations recreate vestiges of Key West's once-lucrative wrecking industry. During the 1800s about 100 ships passed by the port of Key West daily, many running aground on the reef. Asa Tift, a 19th-century wrecker and the original owner of what would one day become the Hemingway Home, tells his story of salvaging the goods of the SS *Isaac Allerton*, which was downed by a hurricane in 1856. Shows run every 30 minutes, daily. Children younger than age four are admitted for free. The Historium now offers a 90-minute Historic Walking Tour of Key West. "Meet" colorful characters and famous faces who helped make the southernmost city the destination it is today.

Key West Tropical Forest and Botanical Garden
5210 Jr. College Rd., Stock Island
(305) 296-1504
www.keywestbotanicalgarden.org

Follow Jr. College Rd., then turn right just past Bayshore Manor, to find this little-known slice of serenity tucked between the Florida Keys Aqueduct Authority plant and the Key West Golf Course. This 11-acre garden represents the last undeveloped native hardwood hammock in the environs of Key West and is the only frost-free tropical humid forest and botanical garden in the continental United States. Despite its proximity to US 1 and a busy public golf course, the garden features exotic and native plants that can be viewed from a series of walking trails and is surprisingly peaceful. The garden is home to numerous birds and butterflies, especially during the spring and fall migration seasons. On any given day, you're apt to see a turtle sunning itself on a log or an egret searching for food in Desbiens Pond or sit in the quite, placid restored Toppino Nature Chapel.

Key West Wildlife Center
Atlantic Blvd. and White St.
(305) 393-4840

A branch of the Marathon Wild Bird Center treating sick, injured, and orphaned animals with a mission to educate the public about birds and other wildlife in the Keys. This shelter lies on the grounds of the McCoy Indigenous Park, full of rare and native species of flora. At any given time approximately 100 animals, ranging from seabirds to raccoons to chickens, are recovering here; you can see them during visiting hours. Key West Wildlife will rescue animals anywhere from the Seven Mile Bridge to the Dry Tortugas. The park is open daily from sunup to sundown. Admission is free, but donations are appreciated,

Mallory Square Sunset Celebration
1 Whitehead St.
(305) 292-7700
www.sunsetcelebration.org

A do-not-miss event during any visit to Key West is the famous (perhaps infamous) sunset celebration. Buskers and street players, vaudevillians, and carny wannabes strut their stuff every day as the sun sinks into the Gulf of Mexico over Sunset Key off Mallory Square. Beverage and nosh vendors hawk refreshments while the entertainers compete for your attention.

From fire-eaters to furniture jugglers, tightrope walkers to sword swallowers, you'll rarely see the same routine two nights in a row. A footbridge links Mallory Square to the pier at the adjacent Hilton Resort and Marina, where the likes of vaudevillian Jeep and his dog Moe and Dominique's high-flying cats delight the crowd.

This daily event, a Key West tradition since 1984, is free to all, but pack your pocket with small bills because the performers play for tips. The fun starts approximately one hour before sunset at Mallory. Check page three of the morning *Key West Citizen* for daily sunset times.

Mile Marker 0
Corner of Whitehead and Fleming Streets

Key West is truly the last resort and here's the proof: The official green-and-white mile marker 0 signifying the end of US 1 is posted at this corner. Have someone snap a picture of you in front of the sign that reads END—U.S. 1. It will make a wonderful reminder of that very moment you finally arrived at the end of your road . . . that's providing some souvenir hunter hasn't made off with the sign, which happens with great regularity. Tampering with highway signs (including those enticing green mile markers) is against the law, by the way. If you must own one, replicas of mile marker 0 are available for purchase in many Key West shops.

National Weather Service Station
1315 White St.
(305) 295-1316
www.srh.noaa.gov/eyw

Weather observation in Key West dates back at least as far as 1832, when rainfall measurements were taken at the Sand Key Lighthouse. In 1870, the first observation station was opened on Duval St. The National Weather Service relocated to different spots during the 1900s. In 2006 a new $5.1-million station opened on White St., bringing the art and technology of weather reporting into the 21st century.

The Southernmost Point
Corner of Whitehead and South Streets

Look for the traffic jam at the Atlantic end of Whitehead St. and you'll see the giant red, white, green, and yellow marker buoy that designates the southernmost point of the continental United States. And standing in front of it, in the street, blocking traffic trying to turn left onto South St., preens a never-ending stream of Key West visitors, trying to capture the moment they stood closer to Cuba than anyone else in the country. Call it touristy, even tacky, if you like, but the crowds seem to love it.

USS *Mohawk* Coast Guard Cutter Memorial Museum
Truman Waterfront, Old Navy Pier
(305) 292-5072
www.ussmohawk.org

This historic floating museum opened in 2006 and is a one-of-a-kind attraction in the Florida Keys, and one of only 55 in the United States. The 165-foot-long ship is docked at the waterfront, beyond Truman Annex at the Florida Keys National Marine Sanctuary's Environmental Center. This unique memorial is sure to please landlubbers as well as naval historians. Launched in 1934, the USS *Mohawk* was commissioned to patrol the Hudson and Delaware Rivers to break up ice formations on these two major waterways. The ship was one of the first to be fitted with sonar and was later involved in 14 attacks against Nazi U-boats while on patrol along the Atlantic Ocean. Tours allow guests to visit six decks, including the radio and sonar rooms, galley, crew quarters, and officers' staterooms.

Guided and Self-Guided Tours

Conch Tour Train
301 Front St. at Mallory Square
Flagler Station, 901 Caroline St.
(305) 294-5161
www.conchtourtrain.com

Some folks might think a narrated motor tour spells tourist with a capital T, but the quirky little Conch Tour Train is a great way to garner an overview of Key West in the shaded comfort of a canopied tram. Tours start at Mallory Square or Flagler Station on Caroline St. Children younger than age four ride free. The tour lasts 90 minutes, with one 10-minute rest break at the Conch Tour Train ticket station, 501 Front St.

Ghosts & Legends of Key West
(305) 294-1713, (866) 612-3890
www.americabyfoot.com

Each evening at 7 and 9 p.m., Ghosts & Legends of Key West leads visitors to our southernmost city on a shadowy saunter down the narrow lanes of Old Town. The second ghostly attraction in Key West (see Ghost Tours of Key West below), Ghosts & Legends meets at the corner of Duval and Caroline streets at the Porter Mansion. Guides share dark narratives of haunted mansions, voodoo superstitions, a secret leper colony, and pirate lore, hitting such "low" spots as the old city morgue and St. Paul's Cemetery. This 90-minute jaunt may put you in touch with Key West's restless spirits.

Ghost Tours of Key West
(305) 294-9255
www.hauntedtours.com

Love a good ghost story? Key West's No. 1 haunted attraction, Ghost Tours, offers you the chance to get an in-depth introduction to the most famous ghosts of our island. Highlights include a visit to the city's original hanging tree. Tales of Robert, a haunted doll said to have been possessed by an evil spirit, intensify the mystery. Disbelief and awe surround the deeds of the German count who dug up the body of his true love, dressed her in a bridal gown, and serenaded her for seven years. Narrated by a spooky, caped, lantern-bearing guide, this 1-mile tour wends its way through Key West after dark and lasts about 90 minutes. Tours leave nightly from the lobby of the Crowne Plaza La Concha (430 Duval St.). Plan to arrive approximately 15 minutes in advance to purchase your tickets, and do bring cash or traveler's checks; no credit cards are accepted.

Lloyd's Tropical Bike Tour
(305) 294-1882
www.lloydstropicalbiketour.com

Lloyd has turned everyone's dream into reality. Since 1991, this one-time hippie who loves Key West will show you "the rock" like no other. With machete in hand, coconuts ripe, Conch shell to entertain, you are in for a charming two-hour trip. His knowledge of the fruit trees around the island is awesome. Oh, yes, you ask about the machete and the coconut? Lloyd will show you the proper way to open one and plays "Flight of the Bumblebee" on the shell! In 2007 he won the men's division with his rendition of Saber Dance in the annual Key West conch shell-blowing contest.

Old Town Trolley Tours
3840 North Roosevelt Ave., Key West Welcome Center
(305) 296-6688, (800) 213-2474
www.historictours.com

Join the Old Town Trolley Tour for an informative, convenient entry into Key West. The trolley stops at most major hotels, handy if you're staying in the southernmost city. Day-trippers will appreciate the free parking at the Key West Welcome Center, where you can pick up the tour. The trolleys depart every 30 minutes, and you can get off at any of the nine stops and reboard the same day. All along the way the tour guide will treat you to a Key West history lesson, full of anecdotes and legends.

Old Town Trolley Tours run daily. For children younger than age four, it's free.

The Orchid Lady
(877) 747-2718
www.eorchidlady.com

Capture the beauty of Key West with a guided tour by the Orchid Lady. You will enjoy a leisurely stroll through historic Key West with an informative trek full of facts and beauty. Visit gardens filled with beautiful orchids and learn from an expert why these gorgeous flowers have bewitched creatures for centuries.

Pelican Path
Old Island Restoration Foundation
(305) 294-9501

Visitors who like to wander on their own should be sure to first pick up a copy of the *Pelican Path* brochure at the chamber of commerce on Mallory Square. This handy compact walking guide and map offers a short history of Key West as well as a suggested route that will take you past 50 of our most prominent historic structures. Most of the buildings described in this brochure are now private homes and guesthouses. Those that are open for touring are highlighted in yellow. Don't be surprised, however, if you can't spot those yellow-and-blue Pelican signs described in the brochure as path markers; many of them have disappeared over the years. Even so, the *Pelican Path* remains relatively easy to follow and is a great way to get acquainted with island history.

Ripley's Believe It or Not Museum
108 Duval St.
(305) 293-9939
www.ripleyskeywest.com

In the Ripley's Key West location, they house a Key West gallery with items from Ernest Hemingway (reading glasses, typewriter, and a shrunken torso) and Count Von Cossel (who stole the body of his beloved and kept her in the fuselage of a plane in his backyard). There is also a Boutique of Weird Clothing showing a vest made of human hair, a giant pair of shoes, and even a pair of Madonna's underwear. And if all that weren't enough, they also have a portrait of Vincent Van Gogh made from butterfly wings.

Sharon Wells's Walking & Biking Guide to Historic Key West
1203 Duval St.
(305) 294-0566
www.seekeywest.com

Historic preservationist Sharon Wells makes it easy for you to explore and enjoy Key West at your own pace with a superbly organized, information-packed free guide that can be found at the Key West Chamber of Commerce (Mallory Square). If you'd rather not go it alone, Wells also offers personally guided tours called Island City Strolls ($$$). Space is limited on all guided tours, and reservations are required. Call for prices and tour times.

Wild Dolphin Adventures
William St.,
Old Historic Key West Bight
(305) 304-8000, (866) 296-3737
www.wilddolphinadventures.com

Relax and get away from the crowds of Key West: Take an adventure on the *Coral Reefer* out onto the Gulf of Mexico and interact with beautiful wild Atlantic bottlenose dolphins. This is an ecology tour watching a Key West resident pod of dolphins in their natural habitat where they live and play. On your outing you will see local marine life, birds, coral reefs, sponges, 'rays, and more. Snorkeling is also available on these trips.

Outdoor Recreation

First-time visitors to the Keys who expect to find soft, white, endless sand along the ocean are bound to be disappointed. The coral reef protects the Keys from the pounding surf that grinds other shorelines into sand, and so most of the sand here must be carted in by the truckload. Nevertheless, if stretching out in the sand tops your recreational must-do list, humans and nature have teamed up here to bring you a stretch or two. Some of the parks and beaches charge admission fees, and most have specific hours of accessibility.

Beaches and Public Parks

Bayview Park
Truman Ave. and Jose Martí Drive

You will definitely notice Bayview Park if you are driving into Key West on North Roosevelt Blvd., which becomes Truman Ave. On your left as the road narrows and you head into Old Town, Bayview Park is one of the few free green spots still left in Key West. Look for the gazebo. Several picnic tables are strewn throughout the park and come highly recommended for a shady afternoon lunch.

Fort Zachary Taylor Historic State Park
Truman Annex at the end of Southard St.
www.forttaylor.org

Look to the left of the brick fort for a pleasant, although rocky, beach with picnic tables and barbecue grills. The locals call this place "Fort Zach"; this is where they come in droves to sunbathe and snorkel. The water is clear and deep, and you're likely to see many colorful fish congregating around the limestone-boulder breakwater islands constructed just offshore. When it gets too hot on the beach, head for the shade—there's plenty of it available under the lofty pine trees in the picnic area. The beach area is open 8 a.m. to sunset. An admission fee to the park is charged.

> Keys beaches do not maintain lifeguard stations. Riptides are rare here, but jellyfish are not. Swim at your own risk and never venture out alone or after dark.

Higgs Beach and C. B. Harvey Rest Beach
Atlantic Blvd.

These twin beaches are so close together they are often mistaken for each other. Higgs Beach offers a playground, picnic tables, and nearby tennis courts. It is between White and Reynolds streets on Atlantic Blvd. The beach is open sunrise to 11 p.m. Admission is free. Rest Beach is smaller than Higgs Beach and is dwarfed by the massive White St. Pier. This pier is a favorite with anglers and dog walkers and is sometimes called the "unfinished road to Cuba." Rest Beach has the same hours as Higgs Beach. Right across the street is an extensive playground called Astro City, a favorite with the kids.

Smathers Beach
South Roosevelt Blvd.

Across from Key West International Airport, Smathers is a long strip of sand that bustles with food vendors, water-sports concessions, and beautiful bods in itsy-bitsy, teeny-weeny suits. Admission here is free, but bring plenty of quarters for the street-side parking meters. If you don't mind carting your beach gear a few extra yards, free parking is available on the far side of South Roosevelt. The beach is open sunrise to 11 p.m.

> **i** For your safety, Florida has warning flags posted on our public beaches statewide. Double red lines: No swimming at all. Yellow: Medium hazard, moderate surf and/or currents. Green: Low hazard, calm conditions, but exercise caution. Purple: Dangerous marine life.

Water Sports

Island Watersports
245 Front St., Westin Key West Resort and Marina
(305) 296-1754
www.island-watersports.com

Personal watercraft and jet boats are available for rental by the half hour or hour. This business also boasts the largest riding area in Key West. If you like, wet suits and goggles are also offered. The guided tour aboard a personal watercraft offers you one and a half to two hours of island sightseeing.

Key West Water Sports
714 Seminole St., at The Casa Marina Resort
(305) 294-2192
www.keywestwatersports.com

A wide variety of water-sports gear is ready and waiting for you here. Feel like a lazy afternoon just drifting? Try a Sun Cat floating lounge chair. Or maybe a Sea Peeper—a two-person glass-bottomed boat—is more your style. Key West Water Sports is also home to high-performance shortboards and quality sailboarding equipment. If you've never tried the sport before, climb aboard the Cat Surfer—the folks here guarantee that anyone can learn to sailboard on this baby. Hobie Cats, personal watercraft, baby-seat bikes, double-seater scooters, waterskiing, and parasailing are also available.

Key West Water Tours
MM 4.5 Oceanside, Stock Island
(305) 294-6790
www.keywestwatertours.com

Ride a Waverunner or take an aerial view of Key West, you can do them both at Key West Water Tours. Take a Waverunner on a 27 mile guided tour around Key West or ride for an hour in a four-square-mile play area. Parasail to see dolphins, sharks, sting rays, and other marine life from a lofty perch. Both activities will be a Kodak moment!

The Keys to Key West
5555 College Rd., Bayside
(305) 292-7212
www.gotothekeys.com

The Keys to the Keys claim they throw the largest island party in the Keys. This inclusive package is billed as "do it all in one day" and even their Web site comes with a warning label: "This trip will wear you out!" The package trip involves Wave Running, sunfish sailboating, banana boat rides, kayaking, knee boarding, snorkeling, windsurfing, and parasailing. Trips are from 10 a.m. to 4 p.m. with lunch, sodas, and water served. Be sure and eat a hearty breakfast before this outing!

Parawest Watersports Inc.
700 Front St. at A&B Lobster House
(305) 292-5199

This enterprise prides itself on offering excursionists the most free falls and dips in Key West. Regular rides of 8 to 10 minutes include heights of 300 feet with one free fall and one dip; longer, higher rides of 10 to 12 minutes reach 600 feet and include several free falls and dips. Most parasailing is done behind Christmas Tree Island and Sunset Key. Single and double personal watercraft also are available for rent. Renters must remain within a limited riding area.

Sunset Watersports
Smathers Beach
(305) 296-2554

This outfit offers something for everyone. Parasailing, Hobie Cats, kayaks, and sailboards are all provided on Smathers Beach. For an all-inclusive day trip, take the "Do It All." From the Key West Seaport, a 44-foot catamaran takes you out about 3 miles to a shallow wreck. From there, take turns exploring with personal watercraft, waterskiing, and just about anything else they can imagine.

Boating

Adventure Charters
MM 5.5 Oceanside, 6810 Front St., Safe Harbor Marina, Stock Island
(305) 296-0362
www.keywestadventures.com

Looking for an alternative to the traditional party-boat booze cruise? Adventure Charters offers half-day snorkel cruises, half-day backcountry nature excursions, and full-day backcountry adventures that combine kayaking, snorkeling, fishing, and beachcombing through tidal streams and along mangrove islands that are unreachable by larger boats. To find Adventure Charters, turn at MacDonald Ave. near Chico's Cantina.

Appledore Charter Windjammer
201 William St.
(305) 296-9992
www.keywestsebago.com

Daily snorkel trips aboard this 85-foot, oak-framed pine schooner head for the reef. The excursion includes a full lunch, a fruit platter, snacks, and beverages, plus beer and wine for after-snorkeling libation. Gear is provided, and passengers need bring only towels and sunscreen. A nightly sail-only excursion includes beer and wine (champagne during sunset). During the high season the *Appledore* fills up quickly; call with a credit card to confirm reservations in advance. The *Appledore* is in Key West October through May.

Danger Charters
231 Front St., Westin Key West Resort and Marina
(305) 296-3272
www.dangercharters.com

Don't let the moniker fool you: *Danger* and *Danger Cay* are the names of the two Chesapeake Bay Skip Jack sailboats, not any situation you will encounter on this adventurous charter. Up to six people board the skipjack and right away owner and captain Wayne Fox assigns one of his new crew as first mate. The fun begins as the new mate learns the intricacies of tending to a sailboat and tacking into the wind. The boat soon travels to the backcountry, where the crew disembarks into three double kayaks and journeys through the mangrove islands. Then the sailboat moves to another location, where snorkeling gear is donned. Finally, after much adventure, the boat sails back home. Excursions last about five hours. Full-day trips, sunset cruises, and specialized bird-watching trips are also available. Call for details and pricing. Their traditional wooden power yacht, *Roamer*, takes you to a pristine reef, where the staff serves you a picnic lunch. Kayak to an out-island in the backcountry and enjoy your yacht-for-a-day.

Discovery Undersea Tours
251 Margaret St.
(305) 293-0099
www.discoveryunderseatours.com

Offering the Keys only "underwater viewing room," which the tour claims is a reverse aquarium. See first hand living coral, tropical fish, and marine life without getting a drop of water on you. Three daily trips on a 78 foot vessel equipped with A/C, a snack bar serving sodas, beer, wine, and champagne on their sunset cruise. The boat is handicapped accessible.

Dream Catcher Charters
5555 College Rd., Bayside
(305) 304-0497
www.chartersofkeywest.com

How romantic for a couple or great fun with a group of six—cruising the Key West harbor in your own personal 29-foot powerboat. Your captain handles all the navigating as you enjoy the company and the lovely view of Key West from the water. The trip is approximately two hours. Sodas and water are provided. The sunset is free!

Fury Catamarans
237 Front St.
(305) 294-8899
www.furycat.com

Climb aboard one of Fury's 65-foot catamarans for a sail by day or night. Fury offers three-hour trips to the reef daily for snorkeling—one in the morning, one in the afternoon—plus a two-hour champagne sunset sail each evening. You can buy separate tickets for day snorkeling or sunset sailing, or purchase a combination snorkeling/sunset sail ticket. Fury also offers snuba excursions. (Snuba, a cross between scuba diving and snorkeling, involves a cylinder of compressed air attached to a raft and connected to two 20-foot-long regulator hoses that participants use for breathing.) Beer, white wine, sodas, and snorkeling/snuba gear are included in the price of your ticket. In addition, Fury offers parasailing as well as a land/sea excursion package that includes a trip to the reef and a tour of Key West aboard either the Conch Tour Train or Old Town Trolley.

Liberty Fleet of Tall Ships
202 William St., Docks at Schooner Wharf
(305) 292-0332
www.libertyfleet.com

The 80-passenger schooner *Liberty* now resides full time in Key West, offering two-hour morning, afternoon, and sunset sails year-round. Sunset sails include complimentary beer, wine, and champagne. Passengers are invited to participate in hands-on sailing, but it's perfectly okay if you just want to sit back and let the captain do all the work. The 125-foot, 115-passenger *Liberty Clipper* plies the waters off the Florida Keys and Dry Tortugas from November through May. On Tuesday, Thursday, and Sunday nights, passengers can dine on Caribbean-style favorites while they listen to reggae music and watch the sun sink into the Gulf. During the summer months, the *Liberty Clipper* offers a variety of adventure cruises along the Atlantic coast. Check the Web site for details. Not to be missed is Joe Universe and his "Stargazer" night sails.

Mosquito Coast Island Outfitters
MM 4.2 Oceanside, Stock Island
(305) 295-9898
www.mosquitocoast.net

The gang at this outfitters offers guided backcountry tours that include a narration of the trees, birds, fish, coral, sponges, sea grass, and sea creatures. Single and double kayaks are available; half the trip is devoted to snorkeling. Gear, snacks, and bottled water are included in the fee. They even have a two-hour paddle tour with you and your dog! Children are welcome but must be at least nine years old to participate.

Restless Native Charters
201 William St.
(305) 394-0600
www.restlessnative.com

Sail away for the day on this luxurious 50 ft. catamaran yacht while you enjoy a gourmet lunch with wine, beer, or soda. Sailing on board this beauty, with her 28 ft. beam, you can expect a smooth and unforgettable time on the water. On board are two kayaks for individual pursuits, swinging air chairs and hammocks, get dragged from the cargo net, snorkel on the reef, or walk the sandbar. The Restless Native can only carry six passengers, with crew, so this is like having your own private vessel to explore the waters off Key West.

Sebago Catamarans
201 William St., at the historic Key West Seaport
(305) 292-4768, (800) 507-9955
www.keywestsebago.com

Head out to the reef for a snorkeling/sailing adventure aboard Sebago's 60-foot catamaran or cruise Key West Harbor at sunset. Complimentary drinks are served on both excursions. Sebago also offers parasailing as well as a six-hour "Island Ting" trip that includes kayaking, snorkeling, and sailing, plus a luncheon buffet. Call for details.

Sunny Days Catamaran
Key West Historic Seaport
(305) 294-7755
www.sunnydayskeywest.com

The 100-passenger, high-speed *Fast Cat II* makes the voyage from Key West to Fort Jefferson in just under than two hours. As a result of the time saved, passengers aboard *Fast Cat II* can get in a little extra snorkeling at Garden Key or even squeeze in a snorkeling side trip to the Windjammer wreck (there's an extra charge per person for the side trip). A continental breakfast and lunch are included in the fare, along with snorkeling gear and instruction and a guided tour of Fort Jefferson. Campers pay an extra fee to accommodate their gear. In addition to its daily run to Fort Jefferson, Sunny Days also offers twice-daily cruises aboard their *Caribbean Spirit*. The excursions go to the reef for snorkeling, a combination snorkeling/sunset cruise, and a champagne sunset cruise. *Reef Express* thrills you with snorkeling in two locations, with half-day outings with sunset combos. Dolphin tours let you go to the backcountry to observe dolphins at play. *Cruzan Cat* puts you onboard a 43-foot catamaran and powers you out, in 20 minutes, to a coral reef. All prices vary depending on the length of the cruise and the time of day.

White Knuckle Thrill Boat
MM 4.5 Oceanside, Hurricane Hole Marina, Stock Island
(305) 797-0459
www.whiteknucklethrillboatride.com

Hold on to your head, keep your arms inside the boat and your feet on the footboards—you are in for one wild ride! This is not a boat ride for the faint of heart nor your elderly relatives. With a velocity of about 50 mph, this boat is a mix of an Everglades airboat and a Jet Ski with a screaming group of about 12 on board. Twisting, turning, and spraying saltwater every which way, you return to the dock exhilarated and soaking wet. A photographer is on hand to capture that look on your face as the "White Knuckle" makes a 360-degree turn—priceless.

Yankee Fleet Ferry to Fort Jefferson and Dry Tortugas National Park
Key West Historic Seaport
(305) 294-7009, (800) 322-0013
www.yankeefreedom.com

A voyage to Dry Tortugas National Park, 70 miles west of Key West, requires a full day. Here you can take a tour of the massive and historical Fort Jefferson on Garden Key and enjoy calm seas, pristine natural sand beaches, and some of the best snorkeling anywhere. The protected waters surrounding the Tortugas sparkle with all the sea creatures of the coral reef, plus a few shipwreck remains.

Do remember, however, that there is no food, fresh water, electricity, or medical assistance at Fort Jefferson.

Golf and Tennis

Bayview Park Tennis
1310 Truman Ave.
(305) 294-1346

The tennis courts at Bayview Park are open to all on a first-come, first-served basis. Reservations are neither required nor accepted. There are no court fees, and courts are lit until 10 p.m.

Island City Tennis
1310 Truman Ave.
(305) 294-11346

These public tennis courts are owned by the city of Key West and keep the lights on till 9 p.m. Island City Tennis is right on Truman Ave. that leads to Duval St. It is first-come-first-serve and is very popular and enjoyed by visitors as well as locals. There is a pro-shop on premises operated by a father and son team that are a delight. In fact, the father teaches tennis at Key West High School.

Key West Golf Club
MM 5 Bayside, Stock Island
(305) 294-5232
www.kwgclub.com

The only public 18-hole course in the Keys, this par-70 course designed by Rees Jones offers a clubhouse, pro shop, and lessons. Greens fees are hefty in high season but about a third less in the off-season. For late-afternoon golfers, special "twilight" fees are available after 2:30 p.m. Monroe County residents receive discounts, but you must reside here year-round to qualify. Call for details.

Key West Tennis Too
811 Seminole Ave.
(305) 296-3029

Affiliated with the Casa Marina Resort and adjacent to it, Key West Tennis Too utilizes the hotel's three hard-surface courts. Tournament lights make nighttime play possible. A pro offers lessons by appointment, you can rent a ball machine, and a complete pro shop carries top-brand racquets and offers in-house stringing. Guests of the Casa Marina or Reach Resort play for about half the court fees that the public pays. Tennis clinics are held daily.

Air Tours

Island Aeroplane Tours
Key West International Airport,
3469 South Roosevelt Blvd.
(305) 294-8687
www.keywestairtours.com

For a bird's-eye view of Key West and beyond, take a ride in a vintage open-cockpit biplane. Tours range from six minutes to more than an hour.

Seaplanes of Key West
Key West International Airport
3471 South Roosevelt Blvd.
(305) 294-0709, (800) 950-2359
www.seaplanesofkeywest.com

There is simply no faster, easier, more incredible way to reach Dry Tortugas National Park—70 miles due west across open water from Key West—than via seaplane. With Seaplanes of Key West, everyone onboard gets a window seat for the 45-minute flight to Fort Jefferson. In addition to navigating the skies, your pilot will point out the sights as you glide just 500 feet above the emerald waters of the Gulf of Mexico. Along the way, you're likely to spot sea turtles, rays, dolphins, and a shipwreck or two.

Arts and Culture

Call or visit the Web sites of the listings in this section for the current performance schedules. The performance season in Key West is generally from November through April. See maps for listings and locations of galleries throughout Key West.

Island Opera Theatre
Various Florida Keys locations
(305) 294-0404
www.islandopera.com

Affordable opera and musical theater. Their repertoire runs the gamut from serious to comedic opera and from dinner theater to musicals.

Key West Symphony Orchestra
1119 Varela St.
(305) 292-1774
www.keywestsymphony.com

The critically acclaimed orchestra of more than 40 classical musicians plays to standing room only at the Tennessee Williams Fine Arts Center on three weekends between November and April.

Red Barn Theatre
319 Duval St. (rear)
(305) 296-9911
www.redbarntheatre.com

Five or six shows each year, including original comedies, musicals, and dramas by published writers. Its season runs from late November through June.

Tennessee Williams Fine Arts Center
5901 West College Rd., Stock Island
(305) 296-1520
www.tennesseewilliamstheatre.com

A full season of dance, theater, chamber music, and shows by nationally known performing artists. It is also home to the Key West Symphony Orchestra (see listing above). Chamber music concerts are sprinkled throughout the copious performance calendar that runs from late November through April.

Tropic Cinema
416 Eaton St.
(305) 295-9493
www.keywestfilm.org

The Key West Film Society formed in 1998 to bring the area the best of independent, foreign, and alternative movies. Since then Tropic Cinema has showcased over 150 films.

Waterfront Playhouse
Mallory Square
(305) 294-5015
www.waterfrontplayhouse.com

Community theater at its finest presents a variety of musicals, comedies, dramas, and mysteries each season.

Nightlife and Entertainment

Renowned for its nightlife, Key West boasts of having more bars per capita than anywhere else in the United States. With many of the establishments open seven days a week until 4 a.m., this tiny island lives up to its slightly eccentric reputation. An age-old tradition in Key West is called the "Duval Crawl"—a sampling of libations from all the nightspots on Duval St., until the only means of moving is to crawl. We recommend a road map for such a crawl: Start at the Atlantic end of Duval St., where the pubs are more sparsely located, and move toward the Gulf of Mexico, where the kegs flow freely.

The Afterdeck Bar at Louie's Backyard
700 Waddell Ave.
(305) 294-1061
www.louiesbackyard.com

The deck is large and right on the water. And we do mean right on the water. One false step, a few cocktails too many, and . . . splash! Service is friendly and courteous, and the setting is exactly what you imagine when you think of the Keys.

Backroom Saloon and Speak Easy
Behind Sloppy Joe's, Duval and Green, Key West
(305) 294-5717

Located upstairs behind world-famous Sloppy Joe's Bar (see page 111) on Duval St., the Backroom Saloon and Speak Easy is another venue in this popular hangout. Large-screen TV and porch seating are available at the Saloon. The Speak Easy opens at 7 p.m. and shows NFL and college football on HDTV. Gives you a little "home away from home" feeling!

Bourbon Street Pub
724 Duval St.
(305) 296-1992
www.bourbonstreetpub.com

Live entertainment at the predominantly gay Bourbon St. includes bands, drag shows, comedians, and, on weekends, male dancers. Key West's only VJ plays tunes, mixing videos with songs for dancing. The emphasis here is on high-energy dance music. Happy hour is noon to 8 p.m. daily, and Friday is the Drag Your Ass to Bourbon St. party, when all bartenders dress in drag and the bar sees its largest crowd of the week.

Buck's Bottle Cap Bar and Liquor Locker
1128 Simonton St.
(305) 296-2807

Not your average cowboy bar. Yep, it may have swinging saloon doors, but with polished dance floors and plush sofas and chairs, this is a swell country-western joint. It is a drinking hole with a deep history of infamous and famous patrons, and just recently new owners brought

American roots music and country rock in for entertainment. Giddyup.

Bull & Whistle
224 Duval St.
(305) 296-4565
www.thebullandwhistle.com

This local favorite is actually three bars in one. The Bull is downstairs and features live music in an open-air setting. The Whistle is upstairs and offers pool and video games, along with a great view of Duval St. from the balcony. The Garden of Eden, on the very top, has a great view of Key West . . . and more. It's the only clothing-optional roof garden in town. The Bull & Whistle complex is located at the corner of Duval and Caroline streets.

Captain Tony's Saloon
428 Greene St.
(305) 294-1838
www.capttonyssaloon.com

Just half a block off Duval, this watering hole with its walls covered with undies and business cards is the site of Key West's first hanging tree—still in evidence inside the bar. Live entertainment nightly.

Cowboy Bill's
618 Duval St.
(305) 295-8219
www.cowboybillskw.com

Mechanical bull and all, patrons are in for one wild ride! Hold on to those cowboy hats—this is not for amateurs! Boot scoot across the dance floor to live music and there is a game room with pool, darts, video games, and TVs.

801 Bourbon Bar and Cabaret
801 Duval St.
(305) 294-4737
www.801bourbon.com

With a clientele consisting of primarily gay patrons and tourists, the 801 offers a first-floor bar with billiards. A second floor offers live entertainment with drag shows nightly, beginning at 11 p.m.; if you've never seen a drag show, you may be pleasantly surprised. The professionally choreographed productions here are loads of fun.

Fat Tuesday
305 Duval St.
(305) 296-9373

Stop in at Fat Tuesday and choose from one of nearly 30 flavors of frozen drinks, including margaritas, piña coladas, and 190-octane rum runners. Our favorite is the Pain in the Ass, a combination piña colada and rum runner. The motto here is "One daiquiri, two daiquiri, three daiquiri, floor," and you can buy a T-shirt that says it.

Finnegan's Wake Irish Pub & Eatery
320 Grinnell St.
(305) 293-0222
www.keywestirish.com

Exactly like a good Irish public house ought to be, Finnegan's keeps the merriment going until nearly dawn (4 a.m.) and is among a mere handful of Key West establishments serving food into the wee hours. Enjoy live Irish music on weekends.

Grand Vin
1107 Duval St.
(305) 296-1020

The tiny bar/wine shop that is the footprint of Grand Vin is a local favorite. Good natured bar servers are knowledgeable about their stock. Limited seating.

Green Parrot
601 Whitehead St.
(305) 294-6133
www.greenparrot.com

Not exactly on Duval St., but close enough and so quintessentially Key West, the Green Parrot rates a stop on any Duval Crawl. Frequented primarily by locals, this eclectic bar is housed in an 1890s-era building half a block off Duval, down Southard St. Walls are adorned with unusual oversize portraits and a wall mural of the Garden of Eden. Weekends feature local and national bands playing blues and zydeco, and the large dance floor is usually crowded. The bar also sports video games, billiard tables, darts, a pinball machine, and a jukebox.

Hard Rock Cafe
313 Duval St.
(305) 293-0230
www.hardrock.com

A world-renowned classic, Hard Rock Cafe is situated in a renovated, three-story, Conch-style house on Duval St. and celebrates historic Key West, the preservation of the Florida Keys' fragile environment, and, of course, rock 'n' roll.

Hog's Breath Saloon
400 Front St.
(305) 292-2032
www.hogsbreath.com

You have to love a place where the slogan is "Hog's Breath is better than no breath at all." "The Hog," as locals know this place, features an open-air mahogany bar surrounded by water-sports-related memorabilia. Try the medium-bodied Hog's Breath beer and sample one of the saloon's famed fish sandwiches. Live bands play throughout the day and well into the evening.

Jimmy Buffett's Margaritaville Café
500 Duval St.
(305) 292-1435
www.margaritaville.com/keywest

Lunch really could last forever here, and patrons who steer here quite often remain throughout much of the day. "Parrothead" and other island music plays in the background, and decorations include oversize props from stage settings of Buffett tours. Specialties of the house include Cheeseburgers in Paradise, blackened hot dogs, Delta catfish Reuben, and fried Key West shrimp baskets. Beginning at 10:30 each night and continuing well into the wee hours, a variety of bands and solo artists perform everything from rock 'n' roll to reggae to rhythm and blues. Yes, the big man himself does play here once in a while, as do some of the Coral Reefers and bands that have opened for Jimmy on tour.

La-Te-Da
1125 Duval St.
(305) 296-6706
www.lateda.com

The La-Te-Da is a combination hotel, cabaret, restaurant, and bar that has been an icon of the party scene since 1978. They offer live entertainment in the Cabaret Lounge and the By George Bar. There is also a Terrace Bar overlooking a beautiful tropical pool.

Pier House Resort
1 Duval St.
(305) 296-4600, (800) 327-8340
www.pierhouse.com

The view of the sunset is beautiful from the Havana Docks Bar; and the intimate Beach Bar & Grille has great entertainment nightly; and if you like things a little quieter, settle in and enjoy the piano bar in the dimly lit Wine Galley.

Point 5
915 Duval St.
(305) 296-0669
www.915duval.com

The bar at this sleek and sexy lounge features is a glowing slab of white onyx; the walls, ceilings, and floors are covered in fabulous Dade county pine; and the furniture is retro 1960. Submit to a Kobe burger from the bar menu while relaxing at your table on the open air porch overlooking Duval St. Located above the chic 915 restaurant.

Rick's Key West
202–208 Duval St.
(305) 296-4890, (877) 659-9719
www.rickskeywest.com

Rick's Key West offers four nightspots in one complex. The Downstairs Bar offers live professional entertainment from 3 p.m. until midnight. And then the amateurs take over until 4 a.m. at the karaoke bar. The Tree Bar allows you to sit and sip a spell, all the while watching the sights of Duval St. pass by. Durty Harry's opens at 8 p.m. and plays live rock 'n' roll until 4 a.m. This bar also has a television wall showcasing all major sporting events. And for a little more risqué entertainment, the Red Garter Saloon is a mirror-and-brass adult club. Pick your pleasure.

Rum Barrel
524 Front St.
(305) 292-7862
www.rumbarrel.com

An active, fun bar and restaurant is located right next to the Pirate Soul Museum, the interior has the aura of a 300-year-old tavern. Rum Barrel serves more than 30 different beers.

Schooner Wharf Bar
202 William St.
(305) 292-9520
www.schoonerwharf.com

Dockside at the Key West Historic Seaport, the open-air, thatched-palm Schooner Wharf, which bills itself as "the last little bit of old Key West," offers live jazz, rhythm and blues, and island music.

Sloppy Joe's Bar
201 Duval St.
(305) 294-5717
www.sloppyjoes.com

It's no wonder this was Hemingway's favorite watering hole. The upbeat atmosphere of Sloppy Joe's is contagious. The bar opened in 1933 on the site of what is now Captain Tony's Saloon. In 1937 it moved to its current location. Some say that Hemingway did some writing in the back rooms of the bar and kept a few of his manuscripts locked up here. Photos of Hemingway line the walls. Live entertainment is offered from noon to 2 a.m. daily. Among the brews offered here is Sloppy Joe's beer, which is actually made by Coors. A gift shop sells T-shirts, boxer shorts, hats, and other souvenirs with the Sloppy Joe's logo.

Splash Bar at the Radisson
3820 North Roosevelt Blvd.
(305) 294-5511

Locals and tourists alike find this a great place to people watch and enjoy live entertainment on weekends.

Stick and Stein Sports Rock Cafe
Key Plaza Shopping Center
North Roosevelt Blvd.
(305) 296-3352

With pool tables, air hockey, darts, video and pinball games, including miniature "Keys bowling," Stick and Stein earns its reputation as the biggest sports bar in Key West. Watch the game of your choice on one of dozens of TV screens or satisfy your appetite with some chicken wings or peel-and-eat shrimp.

The Top
Crowne Plaza Key West La Concha
430 Duval St.
(305) 296-2991
www.laconchakeywest.com

High above the city of Key West, with views of the Key West harbor as well as up and down Duval St., this eagle's-eye perch is one of the most famous bars in all the Keys. Rumor has it Hemingway romanced Ava Gardner and Marlene Dietrich at La Concha and spent many romantic nights high in the sky (in more ways than one) here at this bar.

Turtle Kraals Waterfront Seafood Grill and Bar
231 Margaret St.
(305) 294-2640
www.turtlekraals.com

The lounge part of this turtle-cannery-turned-restaurant rocks throughout the evening, offering live entertainment (in season) and billiard tables in an open-air, waterfront setting.

Virgilio's
524 Duval St.
(305) 296-8118
www.latrattoria.us

This classy little New York–style bar is not really on Duval; it's actually situated on Applerouth Lane, just around the corner from La Trattoria, one of Key West's best Italian eateries (see the Restaurants chapter). Martinis and their cousins—Gibsons, Manhattans, and cosmopolitans—are the specialty here. Grab a seat at the bar or in one of the overstuffed easy chairs while you sip your cocktail and listen to live light jazz and contemporary music from some of Key West's finest musical talent.

Index

Accommodations
Beachside Resort and Conference Center, 14–15
Casa Marina Resort and Beach Club, 15
Crowne Plaza Key West La Concha, 15–16
Hyatt Key West Resort & Spa, 16
The Inn at Key West, 17
Ocean Key Resort and Spa, 17
Pier House Resort and Caribbean Spa, 18
The Reach Resort, 18
Southernmost Hotel, 19
Southernmost on the Beach, 19
Sunset Key Guest Cottages, 21
The Westin Key West Resort and Marina, 21

Arts and Culture
Island Opera Theatre, 101
Key West Symphony Orchestra, 101
Red Barn Theatre, 101–2
Tennessee Williams Fine Arts Center, 102
Tropic Cinema, 102
Waterfront Playhouse, 102

Attractions
African Cemetery at Higgs Beach, 63
Audubon House & Tropical Gardens, 54
Conch Tour Train, 79
Curry Mansion, 55
East Martello Museum, 55–56
Flagler Station Over-Sea Railway Historeum, 64–65
Florida Keys Eco-Discovery Center, 65–66
Florida Keys Historical Military Memorial, 56
Fort Zachary Taylor State Park Historical Site, 66–67
Ghosts & Legends of Key West, 79–80
Ghost Tours of Key West, 80
Harry S Truman Little White House, 57
Hemingway Home and Museum, 57–58
Heritage House Museum and Robert Frost Cottage, 58–59
Joe Allen Garden Center, 67–68
Key West AIDS Memorial, 68
Key West Aquarium, 68–69

The Key West Butterfly & Nature Conservatory, 69–71
Key West City Cemetery, 71–72
Key West Historic Seaport and HarborWalk, 72
Key West Historical Memorial Sculpture Garden, 72–73
Key West Lighthouse and Keeper's Quarters Museum, 59–60
The Key West Museum of Art and History at the Custom House, 60
Key West Shipwreck Historeum, 73–74
Key West Tropical Forest and Botanical Garden, 74
Key West Wildlife Center, 75
Lloyd's Tropical Bike Tour, 81
Mallory Square Sunset Celebration, 75–76
Mel Fisher Maritime Heritage Society and Museum, 60–61
Mile Marker 0, 77
National Weather Service Station, 77
Old Town Trolley Tours, 81–82
The Orchid Lady, 82
Pelican Path, 82
The Pirate Soul Museum, 61–62
Ripley's Believe It or Not Museum, 83
San Carlos Institute, 62
Sharon Wells's Walking & Biking Guide to Historic Key West, 83
The Southernmost Point, 78
USS *Mohawk* Coast Guard Cutter Memorial Museum, 78–79
Wild Dolphin Adventures, 84
Wrecker's Museum, 63

Nightlife and Entertainment
The Afterdeck Bar at Louie's Backyard, 103
Backroom Saloon and Speak Easy, 103–4
Bourbon Street Pub, 104
Buck's Bottle Cap Bar and Liquor Locker, 104–5
Bull & Whistle, 105
Captain Tony's Saloon, 105
Cowboy Bill's, 105–6
801 Bourbon Bar and Cabaret, 106
Fat Tuesday, 106
Finnegan's Wake Irish Pub & Eatery, 42, 106–7
Grand Vin, 107
Green Parrot, 107
Hard Rock Cafe, 107–8
Hog's Breath Saloon, 28, 108
Jimmy Buffett's Margaritaville Café, 28, 108

La-Te-Da, 109
Pier House Resort, 109
Point 5, 109–10
Rick's Key West, 110
Rum Barrel, 110
Schooner Wharf Bar, 111
Sloppy Joe's Bar, 111
Splash Bar at the Radisson, 111–13
Stick and Stein Sports Rock Café, 113
The Top, 113
Turtle Kraals Waterfront Seafood Grill and Bar, 32, 114
Virgilio's, 114

Outdoor Recreation
Adventure Charters, 90
Appledore Charter Windjammer, 91
Bayview Park, 85
Bayview Park Tennis, 98
Danger Charters, 91–92
Discovery Undersea Tours, 92
Dream Catcher Charters, 92–93
Fort Zachary Taylor Historic State Park, 85
Fury Catamarans, 93
Higgs Beach and C. B. Harvey Rest Beach, 85–86
Island Aeroplane Tours, 100
Island City Tennis, 98–99
Island Watersports, 87–88
Key West Golf Club, 99
Key West Tennis Too, 99–100
Key West Water Sports, 88
Key West Water Tours, 88
The Keys to Key West, 89
Liberty Fleet of Tall Ships, 93–94
Mosquito Coast Island Outfitters, 94–95
Parawest Watersports Inc., 89
Restless Native Charters, 95
Seaplanes of Key West, 100
Sebago Catamarans, 95
Smathers Beach, 86
Sunny Days Catamaran, 96–97
Sunset Watersports, 90
White Knuckle Thrill Boat, 97–98
Yankee Fleet Ferry to Fort Jefferson and Dry Tortugas National Park, 98

Restaurants
A&B Lobster House, 23
Alonzo's Oyster Bar, 23
Ambrosia Japanese Restaurant, 39

Antonia's Restaurant, 40
Azur, 40
Bagatelle, 32
Banana Cafe, 41
Better Than Sex Dessert Café, 47
Bistro 245, 33
Blond Giraffe, 47
Blue Heaven, 24–25
B.O.'s Fish Wagon, 25
The Café, 47
Cafe Marquesa, 33
Camille's Restaurant, 25–26
The Coffee and Tea House of Key West, 48
Coffee Plantation, 48
Cole's Peace Artisan Bakery, 48
Commodore Waterfront Steakhouse, 29–30
Conch Republic Seafood Company, 26
The Continent Abbondanza, 41
Croissants de France, 48
Damn Good Food To-Go, 48
Dennis Island Café, 50
El Meson de Pepe, 41–42
El Siboney, 42
Fausto's Food Palace, 50
Finnegan's Wake Irish Pub & Eatery, 42, 106–7

5 Brothers, 50
Flamingo Crossing, 51
The Grand Café, 42–43
Guy Harvey's Island Grill, 26–27
Half Shell Raw Bar, 27
Harbour View Café, 33–34
Harpoon Harry's, 27–28
Hog's Breath Saloon, 28, 108
Hot Tin Roof, 34
Jimmy Buffett's Margaritaville Café, 28, 108
Jose's Cantina, 43
Kelly's Caribbean Bar, 28
Kermit's Key West Key Lime Shoppe, 51
Key West Key Lime Pie Company, 51
Key West Tea & Coffee, 51–52
Kyushu Japanese Restaurant, 43–44
La Trattoria, 44
Latitudes Beach Cafe, 34–35
Lobo's Grill, 29
Louie's Backyard, 35–37
Mam's Best Food, 52
Mangia Mangia, 44–45
Martin's Cafe Restaurant, 45
Mattheessen's 4th of July Ice Cream Parlor, 52
Michaels, 30

Nicola Seafood, 37
nine one five, 37–38
Origami Japanese Restaurant, 45
Paradise Café, 29
Pepe's Cafe & Steak House, 31
Peppers of Key West, 52
Pisces, 45–46
Prime Steakhouse, 31
Rooftop Cafe, 38
Salute, 53
Sandy's Café, 53
Santiago's Bodega, 46
Sarabeth's, 46–47
Seven Fish, 38–39
Square One, 39
Strip House, 32
Sugar Apple Natural Foods, 53
Turtle Kraals Waterfront Seafood Grill and Bar, 32, 114

Transportation
Adventure Scooter & Bicycle Rentals, 10
Airport Cab Company, 13
American Eagle, 6
The Bicycle Center, 10
Bike Shop, 10
Bone Island Cycle, 10
Cape Air, 6
Continental Connection, 6–7
Delta Air Lines, 7
Eaton Bikes, 10
Five 6's Cab Company, 13
Friendly Cab Company, 13
Island Bicycles & Skateboards, 10
Key West Department of Transportation (KWDOT), 11–12
Moped Hospital, 10–11
Paradise Rentals, 11
Randall J's Scooter Rentals, 11
Trolley Tour, 12
Tropical Bicycle Rentals, 11
USAir Express, 7

The prices and rates in this guidebook were confirmed at press time. We recommend, however, that you call establishments before traveling to obtain current information.

Copyright © 2010 by Morris Book Publishing, LLC

ALL RIGHTS RESERVED. No part of this book may be reproduced or transmitted in any form by any means, electronic or mechanical, including photocopying and recording, or by any information storage and retrieval system, except as may be expressly permitted in writing from the publisher. Requests for permission should be addressed to Globe Pequot Press, Attn: Rights and Permissions Department, P.O. Box 480, Guilford, CT 06437.

Insiders' Guide is a registered trademark of Morris Book Publishing, LLC.

This PopOut product, its associated machinery and format use, whether singular or integrated within other products, is subject to worldwide patents granted and pending, including EP1417665, CN ZL02819864.6, and CN ZL02216471.5. All rights reserved including design, copyright, trademark, and associated intellectual property rights. PopOut is a registered trademark.

Written by: Nancy Toppino; Layout: Joanna Beyer; Design: Diana Nuhn; Photos: © Shutterstock; PopOut maps: Maps created by Design Maps Inc. © Morris Book Publishing, LLC.

Library of Congress Cataloging-in-Publication Data
is available on file.

ISBN 978-0-7627-5321-5

Printed in China

10 9 8 7 6 5 4 3 2 1

To buy books in quantity for corporate use
or incentives, call **(800) 962-0973**
or e-mail **premiums@GlobePequot.com**.